ETHIOPIA
THE LAND OF PROMISE

AMS PRESS

NEW YORK

ETHIOPIA
THE LAND OF PROMISE

A Book With a Purpose

BY

CLAYTON ADAMS, pseud.

Charles Henry Holmes

Ethiopia shall soon stretch out her hands.—PSALMS LXVIII: 31

So let it be. In God's own might
We gird us for the coming fight.
And, strong in Him whose cause is ours
In conflict with unholy powers,
We grasp the weapons He has given—
The light, and truth, and love of heaven.
—WHITTIER.

THE COSMOPOLITAN PRESS

440 FOURTH AVE. NEW YORK

1917

Library of Congress Cataloging in Publication Data

Holmes, Charles Henry, 1874–
    Ethiopia, the land of promise.

    I.   Title.
PZ3.H7297Et5   [PS3515.O434]   813'.5'2   75-158224
ISBN 0-404-00133-5

Trim size of original edition: 5x7 5/16"
Trim size of AMS edition: 5 1/2 x 8 1/2"

From the edition of 1917, New York
First AMS edition published in 1973
Manufactured in the United States of America

AMS PRESS INC.
NEW YORK, N.Y. 10003

PREFACE

In presenting this book to the world, I am actuated both by humanitarian motives and by the desire to place the members of the much-abused Ethiopian race on the stage of human existence as actors in the powerful drama of life, showing them herein to be men and women endowed with hearts as feeling, with motives as pure, and with aims as high as are those that govern the acts of the children of other races.

The incidents depicted in the following pages,— incidents that illustrate the relations between the white people and the black,— are unmarred by any touch of exaggeration. Indeed, I have simply reproduced these incidents from actual occurrences; and, far from their being overdrawn and luridly colored, the fault has been found with them that I have softened the abhorrence of the reality.

All are familiar with the events attending the riots in different parts of " Unionland,"— particularly in Atlanta, Springfield, New Orleans, and in certain towns in Mississippi and Oklahoma, to mention but a few places. All are aware, too, of the disarming of the blacks by the militia; and the lynching of women and the burning of men of the Ethiopian race are matters too familiar to excite comment. Furthermore, there are other conditions existing, the acceptance of which has ceased to arouse the world's wonderment: the peonage system, the insecurity of life for the " Ethiop," and the total lack of application of the law of the land when one of this race happens to be the victim of man's inhumanity to man.

PREFACE

I have herein carefully avoided the portraying of improper relations between the sexes of the white race and the black, except in such cases as go to show that the " Ethiop " woman is regarded as " legitimate prey," to quote the public boast of " Magnolia." The case of the minister's daughter, who caused the incineration of Allan Dune, is quite within the region of possibility. Endowed with the glowing temperament that marks the people of that region, the men feel their passions fanned to consuming flame at the thought of an injury wrought on one of their women; and the knowledge of this puts into the hands of these women a dangerous weapon that may be used against the black man in case either of personal spite or petty revenge.

It is in the earnest hope that, by bringing certain alarming conditions to the attention of the world, the enlightened members of each of the races will do their best to ameliorate them by diffusing more freely the light of education and culture; and to that end I have set down in the following pages the plans of the " Decemvirate." Some of my more serious critics may question the success of the experiments that Donald Bleeker tried in his laboratory; but the possibility of the ultimate perfection of his idea cannot be discounted.

And now, one final word on the most subtle of fallacies (an argument that keeps in error the black race as well as the white), the process of reasoning that makes the white man assume that his dominance is so firmly entrenched behind the bulwark of prejudice as to preclude any success on the part of the black man to assault it by attempting to enjoy the privileges of a sovereign citizen,— an attempt that the white man looks upon as an impudent effort to establish

PREFACE

social equality. And in this belief he is, unfortunately, fortified by some of the blacks themselves, who refrain from asserting their rights of citizenship because of a certain fear of a violation of their sense of independence, manhood, and self-respect. To the contrary, these blacks should be taught that such assertion of their rights would tend the more firmly to establish their claim to these very qualities.

However all this may be, one can only speculate on the growing policy of segregation. And whether or not the " Decemvirate " may furnish the key to the situation, the fact remains that no intelligent, awakened people may long be deprived of the fullest and most complete title to the enjoyment of life, liberty, and unalloyed happiness.

CLAYTON ADAMS.

CONTENTS

CHAPTER I

THE MYSTIC GATHERING

Ephraim Johnston was a colored barber, who, in addition to his tonsorial activities, conducted a rooming house directly above his parlors,— a modest establishment at 5 Lasalle Street, Cargo City, a large and thriving metropolis of Unionland.

It was Saturday, the fifth of May. As the customers came into the parlors they would greet the barber; but the accustomed jovial response was not forthcoming. Ephraim was troubled. He had had a dream.

Of course Ephraim had had dreams before; but this one stuck to him; and although he was not a believer in visions and hoodoos and bad-luck signs, this dream fretted him for the reason that he could not throw off the spell that it had cast over him. Every now and then he would surprise himself furtively watching the clock.

Suddenly four o'clock pealed out from a nearby church tower; and as it did so Ephraim's three assistants, who, with no little concern, had marked his preoccupation for the past five days, noticed that his face lit up with all the animation of expectancy. Turning away from his recent profitless occupation of cleaning his fingernails and gazing into space, he donned a white jacket, preparatary to resuming his labors.

For days the boys in the shop had been expending

their fund of witticisms on Ephraim's peculiar attitude, — for he had been morose, gloomy, and uncommunicative, a condition they had supposed impossible for him, — and by this time their store of humor was almost exhausted. With relief they now watched him whet his razor with all his old-time celerity, and they leaned forward eagerly as he volunteered the remark:

"Well, boys; we'll know in an hour."

The voicing of this meager explanation was accompanied by a look that showed that the speaker was laboring under great excitement. Breathing a sigh of relief, though he still thought it wise to approach Ephraim cautiously, his first assistant asked deprecatingly:

"Will know what?"

"Will know — er — er — whether there's anything to this business that's been ailing me," returned the barber, still unwilling to confess his dream.

"What's the matter, Eph?" queried a customer. "Been trying to buck the oil trust, or have you got spondulitis?"

"If you'd have seen him the last five days, you'd have thought he was Sherlock Holmes working on some fine-spun theory," laughed one of the assistants.

"By the way, Jack, where is Number 5?" asked Eph, addressing his shop boy. His query referred to a roomer occupying that number.

"Oh, he's in his room, reading,— just as he's been doing for the past five days. Funny way to hunt a job!" was the boy's comment as he closed his remarks; which comment was met by a stern glance from the boss.

Eph was touchy on the subject of this one of his lodgers, for it seemed to him that in some way Number 5 was connected with his dream. The young man had presented himself to Eph a few days before this Saturday, giving his name as Allan Dune and telling the proprietor of the lodging house that he was in search of employment. As Eph, in order to accommodate him, had given him the best room in the house,— from which for the purpose he had displaced an old and reliable occupant,— and to the neglect of his business had gone about the city with this new lodger, the boys in the shop had dubbed him "The Mystic." However, there was nothing remarkable in the appearance of the stranger, who was a man of medium height, of athletic build, black in color, and possessing a very intelligent face.

All at once the attention of the occupants of the shop was concentrated on the patron who now entered. He was a tall, portly mulatto, of commanding presence, dressed in clerical garb. An expression of uncertainty was visible on his well-bred face; but, seemingly reassured by the character of the establishment, his composure returned, and with a "Good-evening," addressed to no one in particular, he took his seat in the line of waiting customers.

"That's Bishop Adolph G. Mangus,— you know,— the one that's just had an interview with the President," whispered someone. And so it proved to be.

Eph's chest swelled with visible pride when he became aware of how notable a personage had sought his humble parlors, and he deftly turned his conversation into political channels, displaying in his talk considerable insight into passing events. He had just reached an interesting point in his discourse on the motives of one of the national party leaders and had at length succeeded in attracting the attention of the

Bishop, when he was rudely interrupted by the remark:
" What do you know about Roseburg? "

And Eph turned to see Jacob Whiteside, a railway
porter in uniform,— a broad-shouldered, good-natured
son of Africa, who traveled from coast to coast. At
first Eph was nettled; but his vexation quickly van-
ished, and with a hearty hand-shake he greeted the
newcomer, for he was really pleased to see this old-
time friend. He was just on the point of taking up
again the thread of his talk when Chester A. Grant,—
one of the most noted lawyers of his race,— entered
the shop. Though Eph had often seen pictures of this
man, he had never yet met so prominent a personage.
In his excitement he completely forgot the customer
whose hair at the moment he had been shingling, and
only one side of which he had finished. He had, however, only time to mark the forceful, self-satisfied air
of his eminent patron, and to respond to his calm
" Good-evening, gentlemen," when from the church-
tower the clock again began to toll.

One! Two! Three! Four! Five!

Simultaneously with the last stroke of the clock the
door that hid the stairway leading from the shop to the
rooms above swung open, and the athletic figure of
Allan Dune, The Mystic, stood in the opening. Instantly the hum and buzz of conversation that filled the
busy shop was hushed as if by some preconcerted signal, and, without any apparent cause,— for the opening of the door was a matter usually of no significance,
— all eyes seemed to be focussed on the figure standing there in the doorway. In the calmest tones imag-
inable,— tones, however, that seemed pregnant with
hidden meaning,— Allan Dune asked:

" Gentlemen, are you *ready?* "

In the breathless silence that greeted the question Bishop Adolph G. Mangus the churchman, Jacob Whiteside the porter, Chester A. Grant the eminent jurist, and Ephraim Johnston the barber solemnly and, as it were, mechanically placed themselves in single file behind the figure of Allan Dune, who had turned and was leading the way to the story above. When Eph, who was the last man in the line, reached the door, although he had forgotten his half-finished customer, he recalled the promise of enlightening his friends, which he had given an hour before.

With his form silhouetted in the doorway and beads of sweat pouring from his brow, with bated breath, with dazed air, and with awed voice, he said fervently:

" My God, boys; it's true! — boys, it's true! "

But this cryptic remark, far from explaining, only added to the mystification of those whose eyes followed Eph's form as it disappeared up the stairway.

CHAPTER II

THE DREAMERS

It was indeed a strange sight to see these intelligent, sober men solemnly mounting the stairs in this unusual rendezvous, bent on an unknown mission,— men, too, who had made their way in the world by their ability to present the profoundest reasons for each act and the keenest logic for its expression. Something of this feeling seemed to possess each of the group as he entered the well-appointed room; seemed, too, to tinge his manner with a certain embarrassment, with the exception of Allan Dune.

Perfectly at ease, he invited his guests to be seated. There was no uncertainty in his tone; his manner was that of a man sure of his ground.

A moment's awkward silence ensued, during which each member of the gathering was wondering what the next development would be. The momentary suspense was presently relieved by the even tones of Allan Dune, who was evidently a born leader of men.

" When a number of men of our race is gathered together," he began, " it seems wholly unnecessary to ask what subject shall be discussed."

And as he paused before continuing, a smile broke over the countenance of each of his audience, while Whiteside the porter murmured mechanically:

" The Race Question, of course."

" Now, gentlemen," continued Dune, " we have been

discussing this question for nearly a half-century. And perhaps it is just as well that we did little else than discuss while we endured untold misery and wrongs. But now we have gone beyond the point of mere discussion. Do you not feel that a crisis in the affairs of our race is at hand? Has not the time come for positive action?"

There was nothing remarkable in the simple speech just uttered, other than that it was the expression of the thought and feeling of every man present; yet it was greeted with a round of applause, in the midst of which Allan Dune resumed his seat.

Next the portly form of Bishop Mangus rose, and he thus delivered himself:

"Gentlemen, in my travels I have excellent opportunity to note the terrible ordeal through which my people are passing and to observe the retarding and blighting effect of Race Hatred upon the future development of the colored race. I have thought long and prayerfully on the subject. We must not lose sight of the fact that we are citizens of Unionland, protected by the Constitution; and, while our wrongs are many and grievous to be borne, is it not well to put our trust in the Lord, until He in His wisdom shall change the hearts of men, so that they will enforce those laws that are just and will cease to enact unjust laws?"

Evidently the Bishop's sentiments did not meet with the hearty approval of the assembled men, for there was an expression almost of anger on Eph's face as he rose and said:

"No one doubts the power of the Lord to make all things right. But for any race or people to sit supinely by, in calm submission to a multitude of wrongs, is to

paralyze every action tending toward the betterment
of that race.   Who can tell me of any reform that has
been wrought by traveling along the line of the least
resistance?"

And, with a gesture of impatience, Eph resumed his
seat.

"I have been thinking "— it was Chester A. Grant
speaking —" how this strangely assorted crowd happened to come here.   You talk of discussing —"

"Do you know, I have been thinking the same
thing?" interrupted Whiteside the porter.   "I can
see that all of you seem to be hiding something, but I
don't mind telling you that I was brought here by a
dream."

"A dream!" echoed his hearers in chorus, whereupon there was a burst of hearty laughter.

"Yes, sir; a dream," repeated Whiteside, undaunted
by the others' mirth.

"Let's hear your dream," was the attorney's request.

"It was five months ago," began Whiteside, "when
I first had this dream; and on the fifth day of every
month since that time it has been repeated.   It seemed
that I was in an immense gathering of my people;
bands were playing, soldiers were marching, men and
women were cheering.   There are many details that I
could describe, even to the recalling of certain faces
in the motley throng.   But there is one thing that puzzled me on each occasion that the dream has recurred."

"And that was?" queried the Bishop.

Whiteside looked at his auditors, and for the first
time he seemed aware of the intensity with which his
words were being attended.

"And that was," he continued, "a banner surrounded by flags and bunting, on which were blazoned

emblems I have never before seen. And upon this banner was inscribed something in letters of gold. Of this inscription I could see the first and last letters; but the form of a man, who bears a marked resemblance to one I have since seen, prevented my discerning the intervening ones."

Here the speaker paused and gazed intently at the figure of Allan Dune, then resuming: "I would on each occasion wake myself by reaching for this elusive form, in an effort to push him aside. On one occasion I shoved my better half out of bed upon her nose, and she brought me to my senses by a rap on the cranium; and at another time, while out on my run, I pulled a pitcher of ice water over on myself. The way I yelled, everybody thought that robbers had boarded the train. Three days ago, while bowling westward across the plains of Arvada, we were within a mile of a siding where we were to meet an east-bound train, when the full force of my dream seemed to be accentuated. Without any previous thought or arrangement, I yielded to an irresistible impulse. I felt that I must be in Cargo City by the night of the fifth. I had to catch this east-bound train. Without considering the absurdity of the request, I asked my conductor's permission to return. I told him that I was forced to get back, but gave him no reason. He promptly informed me that I was crazy, and I was willing to agree with him; but I had no time to parley, as the train was at hand. Leaving a large list of wealthy and open-handed passengers in my car, I grabbed my bag and swung on the train going in the opposite direction. I arrived in the city this afternoon, and here I am."

"And the letters?" queried Grant.

"The letters," answered Whiteside, "were 'E——A,'— the only two that I could see."

"The mentioning of the letters in connection with a dream presents a peculiar coincidence with an experience of my own." It was the lawyer speaking. "I must confess that there was something familiar in the setting furnished by Mr. Whiteside in his vivid description of a cheering multitude of people of the darker race. I had come to Cargo City in the interest of a client. After completing my business, I sauntered down this street until I came exactly opposite this shop, when my dream, which had recurred to me a number of times, came to my thought with startling distinctness. Looking up, I saw the number 5 above this doorway. Without a second's hesitation I entered this shop, though I did so to my own perplexity. There was something vague about my somnial achievement; but I remember in a dazed sort of way this combination, '5 O. P. I.' As to its meaning, however, it is Greek to me."

"There is something mysterious about this whole affair," put in the Bishop; "for I, too, must plead guilty to lending credence to a dream. There is something uncannily familiar in the allusion of you gentlemen to a crowd. But the significant thing is the persistence with which I wrote on my conference list the name of a town of which I have never heard. My itinerary was: April 25, Springville; May 1, Blackwood; and I could not help entering on the list: '5th, Lasalle.' However, after concluding the Blackwood conference, I came to this city,— not by chance, but in a genuine effort to unravel what seemed a mystery."

As the Bishop paused, Whiteside turned to the barber with the question:

" Well, Eph, have you been dreaming, too? "

" Yes," responded Eph; " but my experience will throw but little light upon this strange affair. My dream was largely a combination of the others,— the cheering crowds, the waving banners,— but there was this distinction: this day and hour were constantly impressed upon me, and I have grown actually nervous with apprehension as to its arrival."

" Well, we don't seem to be arriving very near to a solution of the problem," commented Whiteside hopelessly.

" Oh, for a Daniel or a Joseph! " laughed the lawyer facetiously.

" What have you to say? " asked the Bishop, turning to Allan Dune.

" I believe I have a solution," he returned quietly.

" You have! " chorused all the others, rising excitedly to their feet.

" Let us take the letters visible to our friend Whiteside, then let us add the letters ' th ' that followed the 5 on the Bishop's list, and fill in the rest with the mysterious O.P.I., which so puzzled our legal friend, and what have we? "

" Ethiopia! " came in one voice from the four before him, followed by a lusty cheer.

Just then a band in a nearby street struck up the familiar notes of " Dixie," which increased the enthusiasm of the meeting to such a degree that the Irish guardian of the law, who stood idly on the corner, ejaculated:

" Sure, an' the naygurs must be havin' a wake."

CHAPTER III

When the enthusiasm had somewhat subsided, Mr.
Grant the lawyer, who was a great organizer as well,
was the first to speak.   In his speech he proposed the
formation of an organization to be known as The
Union of Ethiopia.   Allan Dune was chosen chairman, and Ephraim Johnston, secretary; the remaining
three to be directors.

The function of the Union of Ethiopia was to establish a bank for the handling of funds, the appointment of agents to take a census of all the black people
in Unionland, the establishment of a publication to be
read by all their race, and the levying of an assess-
ment of a stated amount for carrying on the propa-
ganda.

It was readily agreed that the carrying out of the
plans of the organizers would call for time and sacrifice on their part, and the training of their people in
every way, but especially in the exercise of greater
reliance upon one another.   As each proposition was
offered it was discussed in detail and the conference
revealed many interesting features; above all, it de-
veloped the fact that each member of the Union was
an independent thinker, original in outlook and logical
in his conclusions.

The conference lasted five days, the meetings going

far into the night; and it was remarkable to find what a large amount of effective work could be accomplished without funds. A competent publisher of their race was induced to inaugurate a publication in accordance with the policy outlined by the Union; a request was sent to each weekly publication throughout the country to initiate steps toward the taking of a census, and each member of the Union was himself to urge the formation of subordinate branches in every city and town in Unionland.

There was no attempt on the part of the members of the convention to maintain secrecy regarding its proceedings, and its purposes had become quite well known to the employees and habituées of the barber shop, where prevailed an atmosphere of suppressed excitement, and which was the scene of many vigorous discussions. Jack, the shop boy, had been pressed into service as the page and messenger of the convention; and in many respects the meeting had assumed the nature of a Cuban Junta.

Exciting scenes were numerous during the progress of this convention, and at times these became so serious as to threaten to disrupt it.

In the course of the last day's session the Bishop brought up the question of the ultimate purpose of the Union of Ethiopia, and in his summary of the proceedings he said:

" I cannot help feeling that there is something revolutionary in these actions; and while I yield to no man in my firm allegiance to my people, I am first of all a law-abiding citizen, and cannot be guilty of any act of high treason. I must confess my inability to foresee the final destiny of this people, neither can I see any diminution in the sentiments of prejudice; yet I feel that in some unaccountable way we shall gain our salvation. I repeat to you: Get money; get education, and respect shall be yours,— discrimination shall cease. What you have said amounts practically to a complete exodus and the establishment of a nation of our own. We should remember that we are as yet mere babes in the art of citizenship, and we cannot afford to sacrifice this lightly."

" I am glad of the opportunity to reply to the speech of our reverend friend,"— it was Chester A. Grant, the attorney, speaking,—" for his remarks are certainly worthy of consideration, not solely on account of his clerical standing but because of the grain of truth contained in them. I want to emphasize the fact that these things are distinctly revolutionary; and there is no desire,— at least, there is none on my part,— to disguise this fact, although in a legal sense it can hardly be construed as an act of treason, because it constitutes rather a revolt against an intolerable condition of society. Treasonable acts are usually considered the betrayal of a state into the hands of some other power. And while the term is of wide application, it can hardly prevent bodies of individuals from segregating themselves and controlling their affairs municipally. In such a movement this self-same government of which you boast yourself a part is lending splendid aid, even to the extent of the enactment of statutes compelling the segregation of the races.

" The avowed purpose of an anarchist is the destruction of all law; yet our government regards him as a simple offender in the police court. Your status is altogether different. Your wish is not the destruction of law; it is to the contrary, the enforcement of the Constitution of Unionland, in all its simplicity,— without either evasion or subterfuge. Wherein, then, does the treasonable act lie?

"And, too, the present condition of this people is not an anomaly in the history of nations; for ten to fifteen millions of people to be totally excluded from having a voice in the making of laws for their government is taxation without representation with a vengeance. In the early history of this nation men became patriots by exposing this evil, and those words, 'Give me liberty or give me death,' have come ringing down the centuries, immortalizing their author and placing the standard of liberty and justice even above life itself. When injustice is rampant there is always a call to martyrdom.

"Did it ever occur to you that had Washington and his cohorts failed, they would have been branded,— and perhaps hanged,— as rebels?

"In conclusion, I wish to reply to the claim that money and education will solve our difficulties. I do not believe that that is the solution, as there is not a qualification of money or education demanded by the ruling race as a mark of equal consideration; it is decidedly only one of color. But, even supposing it were a money standard, can you conceive of a race of millionaires? There must always be the common people in an overwhelming majority, and it is these that require our intelligent ministration."

From the hearty approbation that was accorded these remarks it was evident that the sentiments expressed by the speaker sounded the dominant note of that assemblage. Nor were these utterances of the eminent blacks that voiced them the only compelling features of this meeting. Many brilliant and witty remarks were indulged in by the different members of the convention,— witticisms that showed that even those members that followed some humble calling had not allowed their intellect to be crippled thereby.

The chairman acted with the utmost discretion; not taking part in any discussion, but contenting himself with offering only occasional suggestions such as would lead to the most desirable result.

Before the convention closed its proceedings, each member had pledged himself to use his influence in creating a greater spirit of unity among the people of the black race,— that is, every member but the Bishop, who was still in an antagonistic mood. He had always been successful himself and could hardly forgive the other fellow for having made a failure of life. It was agreed that the convention should reconvene in five months, and that the present headquarters be maintained. In the interim a vigorous campaign for an effective union of all Ethiopians was to be launched.

At length came the closing hours of the convention, which were devoted by the members to the pleasant business of becoming acquainted with one another; for each had found that the other was gifted with something noble, something worthy of respect, and a consequent feeling of companionship and sympathy had sprung up among them. Then, after the most friendly of farewells had been spoken, each one departed to resume his customary calling, and the first meeting of the mystic gathering of The Union of Ethiopia had passed into history.

CHAPTER IV

THE SMILE OF THE PARALYTIC

In a humble cabin in the Province of Illicia, Allan Dune first saw the light of day. His mother having died shortly after his birth, he had known only the disciplining care of a stern and unrelenting father. This father had himself been a slave, but at the age of fifteen he had thrown off his yoke,— or rather, had abandoned it by becoming a passenger on the " underground route."

Allan Dune's father had thus grown up with an unquenchable spirit of independence, and had transmitted this quality to his son, who had also by heredity acquired a sort of philosophic strain.

At the age of sixteen Allan had been deprived of all parental support by his father's demise, and, equipped with a fairly good education, had since that time made his own way in the world. He had an insatiable love of study and a great fondness for research, and pored over every authority that delved into the mystery that held the source of all things.

He had early perceived the abnormal conditions and difficulties that confronted his people, and had devoted his life to the striving to alleviate these difficulties. Besides being an omniverous reader, Allan had traveled extensively and was a good judge of men,— indeed, his perspicacity in this regard amounted almost to divina-

tion.   Indomitable of will and impervious to fatigue,
he would, when he knew himself to be in the right, per-
sist in his course in the face of almost certain defeat;
nor was this attitude the result of personal bias but of
adherence to principle.   Generous and unselfish to an
absurd degree, he had never devoted himself to the
building up of his own fortunes.

As to his connection with the Union: he had in
reality come to Cargo City in search of employment,
though at the same time he felt that he was being
drawn there in the interest of what he considered his
great life purpose.   For Allan Dune believed himself
to have been selected by destiny for the carrying out
of some noble and exact end; and often, to his own
astonishment, he had found himself expressing in word
and deed things that were in direct propriety to the
situation at hand, but these words and acts seemed
rather the result of some prophetic power than the
result of volition.   It was this inspirational gift that
accounted for the part he played in the inception of the
Union of Ethiopia.   Never had there been an embar-
rassing *dénouement* to any situation in which he had
participated, if in such cases he had trusted to the
promptings of this inward monitor, to whose unseen
power he had learned to let all mere personal feelings
be subservient.

Until after the close of the convention Allan Dune
made no active effort to secure employment.   The day
following the last meeting Eph sent for him as he was
seated in his apartment.   One of the barber's patrons,
a banker named Morris Bleecker, was seeking a man
to care for his invalid son.   Eph recommended his
new-found friend.

After a short interview with Allan Dune, the banker

sent him to have a talk with Mrs. Bleecker, who was the one to be pleased, and said that he would advise her of Allan's coming.

Allan lost no time in making his way to the address indicated, which was in a fashionable quarter of Cargo City. He mounted the steps of the palatial house with timidity. Simultaneously with his summons the door was opened, and a man of about thirty, dressed for the street, came out of the house. Seeing his ebony caller, his lip curled contemptuously.

"Hello! What do you want?" The tone was insulting.

"Pardon me, sir; I have an appointment with the mistress," answered Allan.

"'Pardon'—'appointment,'" interrupted the young man almost savagely, muttering half to himself, by way of comment: "I hate these educated niggers. Here, Kate," turning to a maid who had answered the bell; "you attend to this." And he strode airily away.

With a feeling of discomfort and uncertainty, Allan looked after the retreating figure; and for a moment he was tempted to abandon his quest. But, seeing the waiting maid, he made inquiries as to whether her mistress were in or not. He was informed that Mrs. Bleecker was waiting for him, and was soon ushered into a cozy reception room.

Mrs. Bleecker,— a tall, well-formed brunette, with handsome features, though pale and slightly worn, as if from worry,— greeted Allan with a friendly nod, a salutation in marked contrast to the one he had received on his arrival.

"Are you the man Mr. Bleecker sent?" she inquired pleasantly.

He answered in the affirmative.

" Have you had any experience in the care of inva-
lids? "

" Not specially; only in a general way," he admitted
frankly.

Then Mrs. Bleecker went on to tell Allan that her
son, who was eighteen, and an only child, while the
family was traveling in the Indian Ocean, had been
stricken with a fever common to that equatorial clime,
— a malady that had left him a paralytic with the use
of only one hand. They had only been back three
weeks, and their physician had ordered them to a
warmer climate. She had decided to go to Savna, a
sea-coast town in the southern part of Unionland.

" Have you ever lived in the South? " she asked.

" I have not," he replied politely.

She knew it; for she had been reared in Magnolia
land, and was unable to detect the slightest Southern
accent in his speech. She felt that she loved what she
termed her " own darkies " best, and she hesitated
about employing him, checking herself as she was on
the point of asking him if he thought it possible to
adapt himself to Southern ways.

Allan, too, was somewhat undecided in regard to the
place, as he did not feel at all comfortable when he
thought of his encounter with the airy gentleman of
the doorstep; and he kept wondering how he could
ascertain his connection with the family. Meanwhile
Mrs. Bleecker was volunteering:

" My son is listless, and he pays no attention to what
is going on. He has to be fed and dressed and he cannot communicate to you his needs, as he has also lost
the power of speech. Sometimes he becomes peevish,
and nothing seems to please him. Therefore, you can
see that one's duties will be very arduous and that you

would be very closely confined. You are unmarried, I presume."

Allan bowed affirmatively, then ventured:

"I hope you will pardon me, but I met a gentleman as I came in —"

"Yes?" Her voice had a questioning inflection. She had overheard the conversation in the doorway and was amused at her companion's embarrassed attempt to broach the subject.

"Is he — does he — er — have any authority here?"

"No"; — smiling —"he is a distant relative of my husband and is cashier of the Cargo National Bank, of which my husband is the president. You will not have to come in contact with him," she added meaningly, "especially if we come to terms; for in that case we shall leave the day after to-morrow. But come; I will show you your patient."

And Mrs. Bleecker led Allan to a vine-covered porch upon which the warm rays of the sun were beginning to make themselves felt. Seated in an invalid's chair, in a sheltered nook, was Allan's prospective charge attended by a trained nurse. Allan and his guide approached quietly and stood in silence, looking down at the patient. All the mother-love beamed from the woman's face; and her spirit of devotion was a sharp rebuke to the modern mother, whose tendency is to relinquish all parental care into the hands of paid attendants. Allan's look, too, as it was fixed on the youthful invalid was one of absorption,— he seemed to be deeply thinking.

"Harold," said Mrs. Bleecker at length, addressing her son, "this is your new attendant, Allan."

The eyes of the *distrait* occupant of the chair met

those of Allan Dune, and a smile broke over his wan features as he weakly lifted his pale, thin hand, which was immediately clasped with warmth in the energetic grasp of the black one.

At this act a surge of color swept over the fond mother's face, and stooping, she clasped the boy in her arms. For the first time in many months her child had shown a sign of comprehension,— a ray of intelligence, — and she was nearly overcome with joy. She kissed his thin lips, crying out beseechingly:

" Harold,— Harold, speak to me! "

But the boy had immediately lapsed into his former state of listlessness.

Then the mother asked Allan to speak to her son again.

Allan, as before, extended his hand, and the hand of the paralytic rested in it with all the trustfulness of a child. At the sight, Mrs. Bleecker turned an appealing face toward Allan.

" Ah," she cried, almost beseechingly, " you *must* remain with us now! "

CHAPTER V

A WHITE MAN'S COUNTRY

After having made a few preliminary arrangements, including an agreement with Ephraim Johnston to keep in touch with him, Allan gave himself up wholly to the performance of his new duties. He assisted with the packing of the Bleeckers' effects, purchased the tickets, made the state-room reservations, and by the hour appointed had every arrangement completed for the departure of his charge and Mrs. Bleecker, and in all showed himself thoughtful and devoted to the task he had undertaken. His employers, who had engaged him at a substantial salary, were delighted with their " find."

The little party boarded the " Gulf Limited " and was soon swirling away across the diversified country, which in its gorgeous springtime attire seemed touched with new beauty and grandeur. Mighty rivers, marshy swamps, high plateaus, soaring hills, and modest dales passed in stately review before Allan's eyes. He was drinking it all in with delight, for in every phase of nature,— even in its dreary aspects,— he always found something to admire. Presently the evening twilight fell over the scene, and later its golden glow gave way before the coming of night's darkness.

Allan's charge had given him no serious difficulty, proving, to the contrary, very tractable and submissive. The mother had directed Allan to administer certain prescribed remedies at stated intervals; which was the only thing in connection with Allan's duties that seemed to irritate the patient in the least. Mrs. Bleecker had retired early, resigning her son completely to his attendant's care, the two occupying their own section in the sleeper.

The night on wheels passed without event, and the party arose in the morning and partook of a hearty breakfast; Allan feeding his charge, who ate with great relish. In pursuance of his duties, Allan was passing through another car when he noticed a familiar face, and soon he found himself clasping the hand of Bishop Mangus. The Bishop was unaffectedly pleased at the meeting with his fellow-organizer.

Sitting opposite the Bishop was a young lady bearing a strong resemblance to the divine,— a girl of decided beauty and superb in build.

" Meet my daughter Elsa, Mr. Dune."

Allan gracefully acknowledged the introduction, whereupon the girl ventured, in a musical voice:

" We have just been talking about you, Mr. Dune."

He murmured something about feeling highly honored.

" Yes," the Bishop assented. " She knows all; but you can trust her," he added confidently.

In the course of their little chat Allan learned that Miss Mangus was returning with her father to their home in Savna, after having completed a course in vocal and instrumental music at Elias College. He also learned that she had won her diploma at another well-known university. But even without the imparting of this information her manner would have betrayed her culture.

Allan informed his friends that he and they were

bound for the same destination; but that he was in charge of an invalid, and begged them to excuse him for the present,— promising to return later.

When Allan got back to his patient he told Mrs. Bleecker that he had met some friends of his own race, who were in another car on the same train; and she graciously agreed to look after Harold for a time, if Allan wished to be with them. Thereupon he returned to the side of the Bishop, and soon the two were deep in conversation on the subject nearest their heart.

"I don't mind telling you," quoth the Bishop, "that there are some good features to the measures adopted by the convention; but of course you know that I am not as yet fully in accord with the proceedings. Now, you must agree with me that the final goal of all human endeavor must be the brotherhood of man. How can this end be attained or accelerated by the separation of the races?"

"I will reply to your question in the most direct manner possible," said Allan, "although it involves the consideration of questions on which many treatises have been written. I am forced to speak plainly. If you will consider, the partition between the races is not a geographical one; it is merely a sentimental one, prognosticated upon the inferiority of the race which is black. In order to prevent the advance of such an equalizing force as culture, education, and so on from being effective in destroying this barrier, it is necessary to have recourse to some other sentiments which will maintain the breach. It should not be incumbent upon me to cite the means adopted. Books and plays denouncing us as 'lower than a beast' are produced; anathemas are hurled at us from lecture platforms and from the highest seats of the government; the pulpit is acquiescent, while the press is vigorously active in endeavoring to brand us all as being ever ready to commit the unmentionable crime.

" Now the result of this universal denunciation is at once apparent. It is the deepest disgrace to engage in the holy bonds of matrimony by these opposite races, and nearly every province in Unionland prohibits it by statute; and yet, unlawful cohabitation,— provided the male is white,— is winked at. The result is public discrimination in every line of activity,— industrial, civic, social, religious. Now, to conclude : Suppose you establish your own municipality. In doing so you would build up a prestige which would create that respect which is so sadly lacking. You would create a spirit of patriotism, a love for that central power that represents us and that is working for our undivided uplift. A people that is respected nationally, regardless of its color, will be respected individually. I speak advisedly and can cite you plenty of proof in support of this fact. When men shall gain the respect of others there will be no contention as to their fitness for amalgamation."

Elsa, who appeared to be deeply interested in the subject, was visibly impressed by Allan's reply. But there was no change in the immobile features of the Bishop, as he proceeded to discourage further argument by saying:

" Really, Mr. Dune, I like to be honest about everything. We will have to admit to ourselves that we are to blame for much of the discrimination and abuse to which we are subjected. Personally I encounter but little, though I am a native of Magnolia. There is a certain amount of discretion that each individual should exercise. When certain privileges are granted us, frequently we abuse them. Hence arises the question as to our fitness for possessing these advantages. There are but few cases of oppression in which a proper display of intelligent action would not prevent dire consequences."

"Much depends, Bishop," replied Allan, "upon the standpoint from which one views his own individual standing. Sometimes by not resenting a brutal kick it will prevent you from receiving another. Should you knock a man down, you could not repeat it if he remained in a prostrate position. From one standpoint I heartily agree as to our capability; for where there is a general submission to unjust conditions, who is to be the judge as to what will be the extent to which this obsequious servility may properly be carried? If a race is not forced to restrain its domineering tactics over another, and if this inferior race shall have no representatives, either in courts or law-making bodies, they become wholly subject to the various whims and prejudices which animate the controlling power. Thus, if we are accorded certain privileges, and some ignorant and vicious member of our race abuses them, it becomes the whim of this controlling race to brand all of these inferior units with the same degrading cognomen as the guilty one; this becomes the verdict, and many of our own people are weak enough to become a party to their own condemnation."

So the argument went on, with reasons *pro* and *con;* Miss Mangus proving herself to be a good listener; and Allan was frequently rewarded by noticing a flash,— sometimes of admiration, sometimes of approval,— in her eyes; although he was speaking only from his heart and not with the desire of winning anyone's commendation. It was plain that she did not share her father's sentiments; but she refrained from expressing open antagonism to the views of this, her only parent, who lavished upon her all his affection and all his fortune. Allan had before this noticed this spark of determination in the women of his race, and had frequently said that, if their spirit were in the masculine frame, there would be an appreciable change in affairs.

As the conversation was about to conclude, Allan having risen to return to his duties, the Bishop, who had also risen to impress upon his visitor a parting remark, said:

"No man of any race will willfully abuse you when you maintain a genteel demeanor. Deport yourself —"

He did not complete his sentence, for a harsh voice in close proximity to them broke in with:

"Hey, you! G'wan in yer car where you belong."

It was the conductor; and he stood glaring at the colored group with the same expression that Allan had seen on the face of his employer's cashier the day he had applied for his situation. Poor fellow; it was henceforth to be his lot in life to see this expression more frequently than any other! He and the Bishop had been so engrossed in their conversation that they had not noticed things in their immediate neighborhood. They glanced hastily about them. Not a black face was visible. Looking up at the entrance of the next car, they saw this sign:

THIS CAR FOR NEGROES

The Bishop flushed and began to gather up his baggage. Elsa, too, understood, and was leisurely packing her books and feminine trinkets, when the con-

ductor, leaning toward her, chucked her playfully under the chin, with the remark:

" Hurry up, my little beauty; get a wiggle on you."

Flaming with indignation, she struck the man's
hand away, as she hissed:

" Brute! "

Allan had drawn back his arm to strike the girl's
assailant, when the Bishop restrained him forcibly,
whispering as he did so:

" Don't, my boy. They'll kill you down here."

The conductor, becoming angrily impatient, grabbed
their baggage and tossed it into the adjoining car.
Elsa, in order to save her father from further ig-
nominy, with a queenly air that marked her superiority
to this type of man, swept past the enraged official.
He, feeling that he must find some victim on whom
to vent his rage, implanted a kick upon the retreating
form of the Bishop, who was following his daughter.

Allan, wild with rage, controlled himself with the
utmost difficulty; when the conductor, with a sullen
glare, said:

" I let you stay in here, young feller, because you
are a servant in charge; but no nigger passengers can
ride in here. You better believe that this is a white
man's country."

CHAPTER VI

THE HAND OF THE LAW

In the stuffy, crowded compartment into which the Bishop and his daughter had been so unceremoniously hustled, nothing more edifying could be heard than the sound of ribald conversation and the clink of whiskey bottles. The seats, nothing more than rude benches, were crowded with the noisy occupants of the coach, every available bit of space being occupied. No attempt was made here to preserve order; and the white passengers on the train, though not permitted to ride in company with the blacks, were allowed to enter there from time to time for the purpose of " taking a nip " from the bottles that seemed to be in the possession of the larger number of them.

Elsa felt that she could expect no protection from her father in the midst of these uncongenial surroundings; for the Bishop, while not an old man, was " discreet." She could not repress a feeling of admiration for Allan Dune, who had shown his willingness to risk his life because of his chivalrous respect for her sex. And as she sat in a corner of the poorly lighted car, screened by the bulky form of her father, she covered her eyes with her hand in pretended sleep, while her fancy roved afield, indulging in those day-dreams so sweet to a maid of twenty.

Meanwhile Allan had returned to his patient. He

was thinking seriously of giving up his position. He noticed that the conductor had been in conversation with his mistress; but Allan could not tell from her manner what the nature of her feelings might be. It was not until he had finished the performance of some duty for his patient that she asked him to tell her of the incident. With his voice quivering with righteous indignation, he related the occurrence in detail. Mrs. Bleecker did not have to be assured that the young man was telling the truth. When he had finished his story she told him that he must not feel so strongly on such matters, adding:

" I was reared in this beautiful region, and, of course, I love it best; but I really think that in some instances they are too severe on you people. You may meet with some conditions that it would be better to ignore. I say this,"— and her voice had in it only kindliness,—" for your own safety."

" I thank you for your friendly advice," answered Allan; " but I would feel less than a man to slink away from such situations."

" I am not quite sure that you understand," his mistress put in apprehensively; " but I want you to try,— for Harold's sake,— to keep out of trouble."

" You may rest assured that I shall harm no one," was his reply.

Mrs. Bleecker felt impelled to tell the young black that it was imperative,— that it was better to feel less than a man, if he set any store by his life, and that the Bishop had done the thing that was considered proper in not resenting the insult to his daughter. However, she refrained from doing so. She was blessed with a fine, discriminating sense of justice, but had never enjoyed the discussion of such questions.

Besides, it was never necessary at home. And she thought of Uncle Abe,— who had been apprised of their coming. He had been the caretaker of their winter home in Savna for years, and she had no more difficulty in understanding him than if he were a favorite horse or other domestic animal. Morris Bleecker's summer home was in the piney woods of Nain; but this season found his wife and son going South because of the opinion of their physician, who contended that, as the ailment was contracted in a tropical climate the change to the North would be too abrupt.

The scenery through which the train was now passing was beautiful beyond description; with wide fields of cotton, in their beautiful pink-and-white bloom, luxuriant fullness of foliage and the fragrance of flowers,— for at every step the perfume of magnolia and jasmine was wafted in at the open windows. All nature seemed at peace, and mankind had only to rejoice in the bountiful gifts of a benign Creator.

The passengers seemed to be in a rare good humor. Mrs. Bleecker had chanced upon a number of friends who were journeying homeward, and all were in happy, animated conversation. Allan was sitting by the side of his patient, who reclined on pillows, his thin, white hand tight holding that of the black man.

Suddenly the train stopped at a small station at which some construction work was in progress. A gang of negro convicts was unloading stone in a ravine over which a trestle was to be built. This ravine was at least sixty feet in depth, and at its bottom lay a mass of jagged stone. In charge of the convicts was a guard of stocky build, who wore buckled about him a cartridge belt and a huge revolver. In addition to this small arsenal he was armed with a heavy club.

With curses that were plainly audible to the passengers in the train, he was urging the poor unfortunates on with their labors.

The stone that was being unloaded was on a flat car on a siding near which the passenger train had been halted. A large piece of this stone had slipped off the pile onto a space on the car that had already been cleared. Calling one of the convicts,— a handsome, slender, brown-skinned fellow,— the guard ordered him to dump the stone off into the ravine. The young prisoner came and tugged at the mass, but he was unable to budge it.

The passengers were watching; it was evident that the guard was " showing off." With the intention of assisting his fellow, another convict stepped down. But, with a curse, the guard lifted his club and felled the newcomer with a blow.

" Who the hell called you? " he bellowed.

The man who had been endeavoring to raise the stone, knowing the futility of his efforts, had ceased trying, but the guard turned to him again and commanded him to lift it. The poor, driven creature tugged until the veins in his temples stood out like whipcord and his eyes protruded. When his strength was pretty nearly exhausted, and while he was still in a stooping posture, the guard, with an oath, lifted his heavy boot and deliberately kicked him into the ravine. Some of the ladies among the passengers turned their heads away in horror, but the men craned their necks. Far below, at the bottom of the fill, could be seen the bruised and lifeless form; and one of the passengers murmured compassionately:

" Poor fellow! He's dead."

One of the women in the car was sobbing softly.

It was Mrs. Bleecker. A gentleman near her, with an effort of consolation, said:

"Don't cry, madam. It was only a nigger."

"Of course,— of course; it was only a nigger," echoed Allan, with a sinister expression, looking at no one in particular.

At this moment the train, which had stopped to coal, resumed its journey, and the incident was soon forgotten, while the humming voices soon resumed their accustomed light tone. It was nearly three o'clock in the afternoon. The train was approaching Savna, which was a terminal. Already the passengers had commenced to collect their belongings preparatory to departing. Allan had placed his charge in his chair and had deposited the hand luggage in a convenient corner.

At length the station was reached, and the scurrying passengers, amid the salutations of waiting friends, went their several ways. The Bleecker automobile,— ordered out by Uncle Abe from the garage, where it had been reposing for more than a year,— was standing with its driver near the curbing; and a wagon and team, with an aged negro in charge, was also in attendance.

At the sight of Mrs. Bleecker and the rest of her party, this old retainer shuffled forward eagerly, hat in hand, and greeted them effusively:

"Law me!" he said feelingly, with a doleful shake of his head; "an' dis am po' lil Harold? He sho was a lively boy w'en yo was las' down heah, nearly two year ago."

Mrs. Bleecker could hardly restrain her tears at the allusion to that happy time; and Allan, in order to prevent a prolongation of the painful scene, hastened to ask Uncle Abe if he had made arrangements to take the baggage. The old man pointed to the wagon, saying that he would load it at once, whereupon Allan offered to assist him; first lifting into the waiting car Harold, who was followed by his mother. On taking her seat, Mrs. Bleecker ordered the chauffeur to wait Allan's return before starting for the Bleecker homestead, which was located about two miles from the city, out on the shell road. A beautifully appointed home it was, situated in a veritable bower of flowers, surrounded by orange trees, and abounding in shady nooks and perfumed walks.

The baggage was quickly loaded on Uncle Abe's wagon, and Allan was returning to the car when he saw a carriage leaving the depot, in which he recognized the passengers as Bishop Mangus and his daughter Elsa. The recognition was mutual, and as the eyes of the man and the girl met, Allan lifted his hat. Then suddenly, his attention was called elsewhere.

Several little Negro boys were playing around the depot platform. A horse that had slipped its blanket was tied to a hitch-ring, toward which was coming a large white man, whip in hand. In childish glee the boys were chasing one another when one of them chanced to get his foot entangled in the blanket and fell sprawling. Rushing forward angrily, the man dealt the little fellow a stinging blow before he could rise and scamper out of reach. Not being content with this, he reached out and collared the lad who was chasing his fallen comrade, and raising the butt of his heavy, loaded whip, he was about to deliver a blow that might have despatched the urchin, when a firm hand grasped his uplifted arm, and a voice in a tone of entreaty said:

" Please do not strike him."

It was Allan Dune, who felt that he could not stand by and witness two murders in one day.

On turning and seeing who had arrested his hand, the man, with an oath, struggled to free his arm; then his left hand sought his hip pocket from which it drew a revolver. Immediately some of the bystanders, who had remarked the occurrence, rushed to the rescue,— not of Allan, but of his antagonist. However, with a deft movement Allan had turned his assailant's wrist in such a manner as to cause the weapon to fall harmlessly to the ground. Though no sooner had he executed this movement than a dozen hands grabbed him, and in an instant his arms were pinioned behind his back. A man wearing a red bandanna and high top boots,— presumably a mountaineer,— had drawn a long hunting-knife, which he was about to draw across the black man's throat, when a woman's voice broke in entreatingly:

" Don't hurt him, gentlemen, please. He is my servant."

It was Mrs. Bleecker, who until this instant had sat spellbound in the face of these rapid developments, undecided what course to pursue; for she had the natural shrinking of a woman of refinement from becoming the central figure of a public affair. As she had about decided to turn her head away so as not to witness the climax of this street brawl, the hand of Harold,— who had taken a noticeable interest in the occurrence,— touched her with more force than had marked its movements since the beginning of his illness. It was at this prompting touch that she sprang from the car and made her plea for Allan.

At her words a voice answered, addressing the crowd:

" Boys, let him go, for the lady's sake."

" Yes," cried several others assentingly; " for the sake of the lady."

But as Allan moved away to take his place in the car the true sentiment of that group of men was voiced in the words that followed him.

" We'll git you yet, Mr. Coon! " cried one.

" Yes," responded Allan's first antagonist; " we'll give him a chance to feel the hand of the law."

Jack Carter, a reporter for the Savna *Times,* wrote a brief account of the event for the next day's issue. It bore the following head-line:

NEGRO DESPERADO ASSAULTS GENTLEMAN

CHAPTER VII

A TRAITOR

If this record were nothing more than a book of fiction, the author would make an effort to introduce the conventional deep-dyed villain and the silly hero, or heroine, who do sensational and foolhardy things in order to create a situation. But being a simple reporter of facts, the author must present conditions exactly as they exist.

It would be only reasonable to assume that in any civilized country when a man lifts his hand in the defense of the weak and helpless he would receive the moral support of his fellows; but here, indeed, was an anomaly. Such an act of chivalry, when performed by a black man, was regarded as the work of a desperado. And perhaps there was a grain of truth in this, if one takes into consideration the inference to be drawn from the threat anent the applying of " the hand of the law." It seemed to mean that that law was the law of the mob, against whose dictum it would be suicidal to combat; and for an ebon character to deport himself as a man was sufficient violation of the mob's legal code.

To speak quite frankly, there is no necessity for the author to draw on his imagination in order to call up unusual occurrences, nor is it necessary for him to invent predicaments in order to present his reader with some sensational development.

Two weeks went by. The little party had settled

down to life amid the new surroundings. Allan would take his patient on long daily excursions in the wheel chair. These outings seemed to be Harold's only pleasure in life, and he would become fretful and disagreeable should anything prevent his little daily excursion. Nor would he permit attention from anyone other than Allan.

These rambles of Allan and his charge, while not governed by any particular direction, always managed to terminate at a somewhat pretentious cottage in the suburbs of Savna, embowered in vines, boasting, too, an arbor, and surrounded by leafy walks. It was the home of Bishop Mangus.

Now, it happened that on the morning after the arrival of the Bleecker party the telephone had rung, and Allan had answered the call. A girl's voice, tremulous with emotion, came over the wire.

" Does a man named Allan Dune work there? " was its question.

Allan was surprised that anyone should know so soon of his arrival, but he simply answered:

" Yes; this is he on the 'phone."

" Oh, I am so glad! I thought they might have killed you."

" This is Miss Mangus; is it not? " asked Allan, recognizing the voice.

A chat had followed, in the course of which the young girl had invited him to call, giving her address. And since that morning not a day had failed to find Allan and his charge at the Mangus home. A warm friendship had grown between the young black man and Elsa, who, though her father spent little time at home, was carefully looked after by an aged woman of the ante-bellum type, Aunt Jane.

At their first interview Elsa had told Allan that she had seen the mob attack him and that she had been greatly troubled as to the outcome. What she did not tell him, however, was that she had made an effort to leave her carriage and go to his assistance, but that her father had forcibly restrained her and had urged the driver forward, away from the scene.

Allan had been introduced into the highest social circle of his people and, because of the prestige attached to him by intimacy with the Bishop's family, had been heartily received.

He had kept in close touch with Ephraim Johnston in Cargo City, and was pleased to learn from Eph's reports of the progress being made by the Union of Ethiopia. With Elsa, who had thrown herself heart and soul into the work, he discussed its different phases and the furtherance of its purpose. They had established a branch of the organization in Savna, to which their people gave enthusiastic support. However, they were forced to surround the movement with secrecy, for the maintenance of which they depended rather upon the patriotism of their race than upon any pledge or oath.

Long and frequent were the conversations that Allan and Elsa would hold on the vine-covered veranda of the Bishop's cozy dwelling, with Aunt Jane just within sight through the open window, busy with her knitting, and Harold sitting not far away in his invalid's chair. Sometimes Harold would show unmistakable interest in the affairs of his black companions, and both Allan and Elsa felt that he would be a sincere and powerful ally but for his infirmity. For the improvement of this condition of his patient Allan had suggested to his employer a different form of treatment, but she would not hearken to it.

To-day the two,— Allan and Elsa,— were, as usual, talking on their favorite theme.

"Of a truth," he was saying, "I know that it was the institution of slavery which created the contempt to which we are now subjected; but I feel that we have demonstrated our capacity for being accorded the same rights as other citizens, both on the field of battle and in the arts of peace. Do you not think that perhaps your father might be correct in his suggestion that we leave these things to the sense of justice and fair-play of the controlling race?"

Elsa laughed scornfully.

"No doubt of it," was her mocking answer. "We have had ample proof of that 'sense' quite recently in our personal affairs, without considering the national aspect of the matter. But," she added seriously, "do you ever think of the little things that combine to perpetuate this prejudice? To illustrate: Little children are scared into submission by such expressions as 'Big nigger catch you,' and so on. You no doubt know of the many little rhymes the children have, such as 'Black face and shiny eye,' and a hundred others, each one breathing sentiments of contempt for the black."

"Yes," said Allan, admiring her keenness of thought; then he added: "And the songs: 'Every nation has a flag but the coon,' 'I wish't I was a white man,' and so on, or 'Workin' like a nigger.'"

"Yes," agreed Elsa, then added with a sense of hesitancy; "not to mention 'that peculiar odor.'"

Both laughed heartily; but Elsa had not finished, for, with a nod of conviction, she concluded:

" These ideas of color superiority are thus engrafted in the minds of the children so unalterably that the entire life is influenced by this prejudice, which precludes the possibility of untrammelled and unadulterated justice in the adult."

" It is a matter for our most serious consideration to determine what attitude to take on the final adjudication of the question at issue," began Allan. " Many assert that general progress and universal enlightenment will destroy the barriers which we have said are sustained by song and verse. Many boast proudly of their Indian lineage,— a dark race,— possibly because the Indian refused to be subdued. It might be premature for us to endeavor to outline a policy,— for example, for us to say that we must establish a similar prestige for prowess. We can safely allow events to shape themselves in this regard. But there is one thing about which we cannot be divided, and that is : Since we are legislated against and otherwise antagonized as a race, we must oppose such discrimination, not as individuals but as a race."

The conversation was here interrupted by the entrance of a half-dozen friends of about Elsa's own age. The Mangus home had become the center of social gaiety since the return of its young mistress, who was very popular. Among these callers was Luke Dean, the chauffeur of Mrs. Bleecker. This Dean had always pretended great friendlines for Allan, but, notwithstanding, Allan distrusted him, never failing to note the hint of jealousy in his manner at the hearty reception that always attended the newcomer's presence.

To-day Dean met Allan with a sheepish look and a suspiciously effusive salutation. The greetings over, conversation became general, until someone suggested a little singing. Music led to dancing, and in the course of the terpsichorean movement Aunt Jane swooped down on the merrymakers with the words, leveled at Elsa:

" Never mind, Missy; I'm goin' to tell your pappy."

At which dire words all present ran up to Aunt Jane and hugged and coddled her until she was forced to recall her threat.

It was nearly dusk when Allan and his charge started for home. On the way to the shell-road his way led through a busy section of the city. On a corner, under a street lamp, he saw three men talking. On his approach they ceased talking and seemed to regard him curiously. One of the men he recognized as Babe Ellis, the man with whom he had had his encounter and who, he had since learned, was a constable. Instinctively Allan felt that there was something up. One of the men hailed him sneeringly with, " Hello, Shine! " to which he replied neither by word nor look. And before he had got out of sight he noticed that the trio had separated and disappeared.

Allan continued his way, wheeling Harold before him down the beautiful shell-road, with its flowered fragrance and trailing jasmine. Occasionally a whirring auto would dash up and away, or a motorcycle, with its popping reports, would go madly by. The two, Allan and Harold,— had gone on to within a half-mile of the Bleecker homestead and were in a specially secluded part of the road. Allan had begun to be amused at his apprehension of danger, when suddenly three shots rang out,— not simultaneously, but in one-two-three order.

Allan sank to his knees, and a stinging sensation

made itself felt in his right ear as his hat fell from his head. And all at once a peculiar wailing cry, like the voice of some lost soul, sounded out on the sweet night air. It was Harold. The paralytic had found his voice.

" Did it hurt you? " he inquired weakly.

Allan picked up his hat and felt his ear before answering coolly:

" Only a pink in my ear and a little more ventilation in my hat."

But he had not seemed to have yet remarked that when he continued on his way he was wheeling a companion who could talk.

CHAPTER VIII

A MINISTERIAL CALL

Morris Bleecker was a very busy man and paid little heed to social affairs. His wife frequently took him to task for his remissness in this regard, but he would always put her off with a laughing excuse. Reared in the northern section of Unionland, and popular with all who knew him, he was not only a successful business man, who had amassed an immense fortune, but was also endowed with an intense love for his family, whose every whim he was eager to gratify.

Thus, when his son Harold, who was an exceedingly brilliant student and had nearly completed his school course, expressed a wish to travel in the Orient, Mr. Bleecker packed the boy and his mother off in a private yacht, with its full crew and a retinue of servants.

The disastrous termination of this cruise had filled Morris Bleecker with the deepest sorrow, for he had planned Harold's business career. Whenever the horror of his son's affliction would come before him his only refuge from the thought was to plunge himself the more deeply into business.

Just now he had torn himself away from his affairs in Cargo City, and was making a visit to his family at the shell-road retreat. His coming brought delight to all, and Harold, who had recently shown wonderful improvement, wore a beaming look of pleasure

55

at the sight of his father; then, too, Uncle Abe's effusive and dialectic greeting was in itself an evidence of the general feeling.

It was but a few days after the thrilling experience of Allan Dune that Morris Bleecker had arrived. On that eventful night of the shooting Allan had brought his charge home and cared for him as usual. However, after he had gone to bed and the events of that evening passed in review before his mental vision, Harold's words came back to him. At first Allan felt inclined to awaken the boy and question him, but refrained from doing so until the morning.

The next day the first words that he addressed to Harold were:

"Harold, do you remember that you spoke to me last night?"

Harold placed his fingers on his lips and whispered:

"Hush! Don't say anything. I'm going to surprise Mother."

On being asked if he had been able to talk previous to the night before, the boy replied in the negative.

Until the time of Mr. Bleecker's arrival Allan and his patient had kept up their daily routine. Allan had talked to Harold and had found that he was heart and soul absorbed in the Union's plans, of which, of course, he was fully advised, having been present at every interview that Allan had had with Elsa. Allan realized that the cause had won a powerful ally.

That morning Allan had received a letter signed "K.K.K." and decorated with a skull and cross-bones, which contained an order for him to leave Savna within twenty-four hours, under penalty of death. The letter had been placed in the Bleecker mail-box during the night. Allan showed the letter to Harold, who was slowly but surely gaining control of his faculties, and the boy's natural bent for excitement was kindled.

" What are you going to do? " he queried.

" Stay until I get ready to leave," answered Allan nonchalantly.

Harold pressed his hand, and again assured him of his fidelity.

Mrs. Bleecker had been troubled during several days previous to her husband's arrival; and while she was immensely pleased at the prospect of his coming, she was not sure that he could mend her trouble, because she did not believe that he would respect the customs of her beloved Magnolia land.

Luke Dean, her ebon-hued chauffeur, who had long been seeking the opportunity, at length told her of Allan's various activities among his people, and represented to her that Harold's attendant had so inflamed the minds of the colored folk that they were on the verge of riot.

Luke had, however, not confined his confidence to Mrs. Bleecker's ears alone; he had also told Babe Ellis, who he knew hated Allan. It had been a great source of mortification to Ellis that he did not " get his man " that night on the shell-road; and the letter that Allan had received was by no means a bluff.

Shortly after her husband's coming, Mrs. Bleecker told him what she had heard concerning Allan; telling him also of the incident that had taken place on their arrival in the city and of the attempt to kill him only a few days ago, which she had only learned from some of the other servants, Allan not having mentioned it. While this conversation was being held, Harold was present.

When his wife had finished, Mr. Bleecker laughed, and his only comment at the moment was that Allan was " a pretty nervy guy."

" Yes," she replied, " I admit that. But this formation of societies among them. You know the authorities have always opposed it, particularly here in Magnolia land."

" I don't blame him," said Mr. Bleecker. " If I were he, I might form a gatling-gun brigade."

Mrs. Bleecker had no desire to discharge Allan; she merely wanted to discipline him,— in other words, she wished him to conform to the prevailing idea of that community as to the proper way of deporting himself. She knew one chord she could yet touch to make her husband act.

" But, Morris, you have never thought of the danger to Harold in all this promiscuous shooting."

" True," he returned gravely. " I will speak to the fellow."

Mrs. Bleecker now left the room to make one of her many calls. But she went away with no sense of satisfaction, for she did not feel that she had won a victory, since she had not succeeded in making her husband accept her viewpoint.

" I know what I'll do," she soliloquized; " I'll make my pastor talk to him."

Mr. Bleecker was about to leave the room, too, when a voice called:

" Father! "

The man turned, standing transfixed, as if he had seen a ghost.

" Don't be afraid, Father. I can talk now."

Mr. Bleecker took his son in his arms in a paroxysm of joy, while tears streamed down his cheeks. When he had regained command of himself, he listened eagerly while Harold recounted to him some of the incidents attending the return of his speech. Then he wheeled the boy, at his request, into a room known as "Harold's den,"— a room that he would allow no one but Allan to enter. To this room even his mother had not the *entrée*. Here the couch, the chairs, even the floor was littered with books and magazines,— all works of a metaphysical character.

Harold told his father to take down from a shelf a small, leather-bound volume, and then asked him to examine it. It contained teachings that Mr. Bleecker had often heard of, but which he had treated with the derision that he thought they deserved. Closely he questioned his son as to his knowledge of it. Harold's answers were so consistent, and were given with so great fervor of expression that his father was greatly impressed; he was amazed, too, at the knowledge of the Scriptures displayed by Harold as well as by his practical and logical application of them.

"How did you learn of this?" Mr. Bleecker inquired.

"Oh, Allan is a student; and he has helped me greatly," answered Harold.

"So that's it?" was his father's comment.

Mr. Bleecker was forced to leave on the following night, but before going he called Allan in, and together with Harold they discussed the subject. It was plain that he was profoundly impressed; for he could see the honesty that shone from Allan's clear eyes and swarthy face, and there was a smouldering devoutness in his manner, though outwardly calm and convincingly intelligent. Indeed, so impressed was Mr. Bleecker that he regretted that he was forced to leave so soon after his discovery of the truth of this doctrine, but he gave his promise to Harold that he would look into this teaching. Before his father bade the family good-bye, Harold had bound him to secrecy both as to his studies and his ability to talk.

The day following the departure of Mr. Bleecker the little runabout of the Rev. Thomas Stickley stopped at the Bleecker homestead, and that important personage, dignified as to air and accompanied by his daughter,— a girl of fourteen,— was ushered in. Mrs. Bleecker received her guests graciously, and they talked of home-mission and foreign-mission work among the heathens and of a variety of other church activities.

Presently Mrs. Bleecker broached the subject with which her mind was full.

" My express reasons for wishing you to call are in connection with a servant of ours. He has become a companion to Harold, and I don't know what my boy would do without him. He has, however, the knack of getting into trouble; that is to say," she quickly corrected, " he does not know how to adapt himself to conditions as they exist here. He neither drinks nor uses tobacco, nor has he any immoral taste. To put it plainly, his great and most serious fault is a desire to assert too strongly the independence and the rights of his people."

" Oh, I see," said the reverend gentleman; " trying to get above his level? "

" Not exactly that," returned Mrs. Bleecker. " Personally he is sufficiently polite and deferential; but I learn that he is organizing societies, the object of which is to place the negro on a plane with the white man."

The Reverend Mr. Stickley's face flushed with suppressed emotion.

"I have dealt with such cases before," he declared; adding the request: "Send him in,— send him in."

Mrs. Bleecker, putting her arm about the preacher's daughter to lead her from the room, turned as she reached the door and said:

"I want to tell you beforehand that he is fairly well educated."

"Yes," laughed the minister; "I know all about their capacity for knowledge."

Presently Allan entered, pushing Harold, who had insisted upon being present at the interview. The black man bowed to the Reverend Mr. Stickley and then stood waiting for the clergyman to speak. He had not been told what was wanted of him.

For some moments the reverend gentleman sat looking straight at Allan, with the palpable intent to intimidate him. He had always believed that the natural superiority of his color would have the effect of squelching any pretentions on the part of any member of the dusky race; but to his surprise he found that his combination did not seem to work in this case; for the man before him calmly returned the ministerial gaze, without any sign of resentment.

"Sit down," came the command presently, in a pompous tone.

Allan obeyed.

"I am apprised of the fact that you are something of a trouble-maker," the minister pursued,— his voice rising as if in question.

Allan essayed to reply, but the effort was vain; for though the Reverend Mr. Stickley had a habit of pausing impressively after each remark long enough for one to expect that he was waiting for a reply, he would check it at its birth with some interruption.

" You will find it much wiser to submit to the laws of our community." Again the ministerial pause; again Allan's attempt to reply; again the raising of the white hand to compel silence. Comprehending his interviewer's plan of procedure, Allan determined to remain discreetly silent.

" You must understand that the people of education, culture, and training are going to rule this country. This is a condition you cannot attain. Hence we will not submit to an inferior race."

Allan, by this time fully familiarized with the other's tactics, smiled as he quietly rose from his seat. Turning Harold's chair toward the door, he looked back just as he was departing and said:

" Excuse me, sir; but I do not wish to disturb your very interesting soliloquy."

CHAPTER IX

LEGITIMATE PREY

A boat drifted lazily, lapping the peaceful waters just outside the entrance to the harbor of Savna. Its occupants were conversing earnestly as they slowly approached the landing. The hour was nearly dusk; and one of the occupants, gazing out toward the receding orb of day, said:

"Well, we must hurry; it's later than I thought. How quickly the hours fly!" he added.

"Yes; on wings of love," replied his fair companion; then she quoted coquettishly:

> "'Thou laggard, far too long hast thou delayed
> The wistful pleadings of a silent maid.'"

The man bestowed an affectionate glance upon the girl, while a faraway look came into his eyes. She looked so pretty in her simple costume of white; she reminded him of a grown-up child.

Allan,— for it was he,— was taking a day off preparatory to his return shortly to Cargo City, where the second convention of The Union of Ethiopia was soon to be held. He had never thought that he would succumb to the charms of any woman,— he had ever felt that he was wedded to his great life purpose; but in Elsa he had found not only a helpmeet but a spur to greater and more persistent effort. In many respects

he regarded her gifts for organization superior to his
own, and her keenness of perception was unerring.
Then, too, she was confiding and lovable.

These two did not often speak of their love, for each
understood how the other felt, and that their feeling
was a flame fed by their unity of purpose.

They had just been discussing the French commune,
with its cry of "Liberty, Fraternity, Equality, or
Death," and Elsa had remarked that the same sentiments when expressed in Russia constituted Nihilism,
adding:

"But what would you call it when breathed in Magnolia land by one of our race?"

"Perhaps the Rev. Thomas Stickley could find a
more choice phrase than I," laughed Allan.

By this time they had reached the landing, and soon
they were making their way homeward in the autumn
twilight. No one, from a mere description, can imagine the beauty of an autumn sunset in Magnolia land,
with its accompaniment of soft odors, the soughing of
gentle zephyrs, and the waving of the tall trees. Allan
and Elsa were enjoying to the full all these delights of
Nature when he suddenly remembered that he was
expected to return to his duties rather earlier than usual
to-night, as the Bleeckers were expecting guests. His
charge, Harold, did not now require so much attention
as formerly, for he was able to move all parts of his
body, though not yet able to walk. Harold was as
urgent that Allan should return to Cargo City as was
the black himself.

Mr. Bleecker was here on one of his periodic visits,
and the guests invited this evening were the Governor
of Magnolia, the Reverend Mr. Stickley,— who was
related to His Excellency,— and the usual bevy of

ladies that serve as a sort of garnishment to every feast in this peculiar land.

But, to return to Allan and Elsa: He had escorted the young girl to within a few blocks of her home, when he bade her adieu, with a promise of seeing her on the morrow. For a little time he stood and watched her retreating form, a great feeling of tenderness filling his being; then he turned and strode away. His mind was full of the thought of the girl of his heart,— of her high ideals, her great beauty, her pure and angelic character, her sweet sympathy for those in distress, and her freedom from egotism because of the accomplishments with which she was endowed. Then suddenly a great brooding care seemed to settle down upon him, even as the eagle hovers over her nestlings. Impelled by some strange prompting, he looked back once again.

In the distance he could see her vaguely through the murky light. He strained his eyes. Yes; she was running. Behind her, at a few paces' distance, strode two men.

"She is only frightened," Allan mused. "They will turn off presently and go their way. No,"— his heart gave a bound,—" they are running, too!"

With the swiftness of a deer he turned and dashed along the way he had just come. He was straining every nerve to overtake Elsa's pursuers, for he could see that they were following her with dogged determination.

Meanwhile, Elsa had reached her father's gate and was entering. There was, however, no one in the house but Aunt Jane, and she was very deaf. The men were following her closely. Once inside the door, Elsa slammed it quickly, but she was not quick enough for one of her burly antagonists, who had put his shoulder against it, which prevented the lock from fastening. Through the crack in the door the young girl could smell the fumes of liquor on the breath of her pursuers. She held on for a moment with the strength born of desperation, and then she screamed at the top of her lungs. She could hear Aunt Jane singing to herself in the kitchen. But the old woman did not hear the commotion; even had she, she would have been of no assistance.

Presently the door yielded, and the two men entered. They were white men out for a lark,— seeking what they considered legitimate prey. Advancing toward Elsa, one of them said:

"What's s'matter, honey? We ain't goin' to hurt yer."

The frightened girl thought she would faint, but, trampling such weakness under foot, she drew herself up and looked about her for some means of defense. A beautiful and costly hand-painted ceramic, which she had herself designed, was on the table. Seizing this as a weapon, she raised it over the head of one. He caught her arm, remarking:

"Don't be mean, baby."

The costly work of art fell to the floor with a crash.

Retaining his hold upon her arm, the man was on the point of embracing her when a swiftly-moving form shot in at the doorway.

"Elsa!" came the breathless cry.

"Thank God, it is you, Allan!" And the young girl breathed a prayer of thanksgiving.

For a moment the two brutes were held in astonishment at this interruption of their pastime; but seeing that there was but one man, and that one black, their contempt prompted them to atack him, and breathing curses, they advanced upon Allan. But he, with a blow of his powerful fist, felled each one as he came up. Then, picking up the prostrate form of one, he was about to carry it out of the gate, when the other one rose and assaulted him anew, thus compelling him to drop his burden and defend himself. The body slid down the cement steps, striking a mud fender at the foot, and Allan was faintly conscious that he heard the fellow groan. He was, however, too busy protecting himself from the assault of the other brute to have any time for enquiring into the matter just then.

When he had finally vanquished his antagonist, who took ignominiously to his heels, Allan turned to Elsa and inquired anxiously if she were hurt.

" Not in the least," she answered bravely.

" I think it will be best," said Allan, " for you and Aunt Jane to spend the night at Brother Stevens'. You can't tell what these fellows might do." Brother Stevens was pastor of the church of Elsa's faith, and he and his family fairly worshipped the Bishop's daughter.

The two women agreed to Allan's suggestion, and locking up the house, they went out at the rear door and were soon at the minister's house. At the gate Allan bade them good-bye and proceeded on to his employer's. He knew he was late and regretted the fact; but it was the first time he had been guilty of tardiness since he had entered their employ.

Allan entered by the rear of the premises, and approaching the kitchen door, was on the point of going in when a negro maid, who had been standing in the shadow, clutched him by the sleeve and whispered:

" Allan? "

" Yes."

" Mr. Harold sent me out to tell you not to come in, and to take this purse and beat it."

" But why? " he questioned uneasily.

" He says they have been telephoning about you and are trying to lay some murder upon you. Now, if I know anything at all about this country, I'm telling you you had better go."

Allan hesitated. He did not care to be branded either as a murderer or a fugitive from justice.

" Hark! Do you hear that? " asked the maid.

" What? " questioned Allan.

They stopped and listened.

" It's Babe Ellis's bloodhounds," was the maid's horrified whisper.

Then to Allan's mind came the thought of the sort of justice he might receive in Magnolia land, and then the thought of Elsa, and last the thought of his great life purpose. The last two surely made the preservation of his life a thing worth while.

And Allan turned and fled into the night.

CHAPTER X

It would require a much larger volume than the reader would care to peruse, if this were to be a full record of the many phases of this strange problem of the races. The universal attempt at oppression, based upon the determination that the black shall not progress nor be enlightened; the tendency to hold him in constant subjection because of a belief in his inferiority as the result of a Divine decree; the peonage system; the Jim Crow law; disfranchisement; the creation of hordes of criminals through a prejudicial application of the law; the silly effort of some physicists to substantiate their claim to color superiority by the presentation of some structural or material phenomenon; the environment of the youth, into whom are injected by his adult instructors all sorts of insidious poisons; the bias of historical text-books, with their glaring omission of all record of Negro achievement; the impenetrable wall of social ostracism; the insinuations of current literature; the song and poetry of the mountebank, who pictures the Negro as either a buffoon or a coward; the passions of the inhuman mob, and the natural inhumanity of man to man,— these are but a few of the many waves in the sea of troubles against which the higher call to perfect liberty and brotherhood is sounding out to us to battle.

Another and powerful bar to equal consideration is

the action of provincial legislatures in endeavoring to shape the sentiment of the people by the enactment of laws that are wholly paternal and subversive of individual liberty.

This was the subject under discussion at the dinner party being held at the Bleeckers'; and there was only one voice that sounded an adverse view from that of the great majority. Mr. Bleecker was saying:

" I think it hardly fair to these poor devils to use the executive and legislative power against them. It seems to me that they have enough to contend with in the hard deal that they get in civil and industrial affairs generally, without this added incubus of governmental regulation."

" Mr. Bleecker is not a native of Magnolia," volunteered the Reverend Mr. Stickley.

" Evidently," returned the Governor.

" He has never seen the great string of convicts of this color as they swarm in the mines and other places of labor; he has never seen the workhouse filled with blacks of all ages,— from almost the babe in the cradle to the aged darkey trembling on the brink of the grave; he has never seen their bawdy-houses, their dives infested with a multitude of criminals, and their crimes."

The clergyman was waxing eloquent with his subject, and Mrs. Bleecker, fearing that her husband had offended their guest, gave Mr. Bleecker a reproachful look. He understood her and interrupted at this point:

" Pardon me, Dr. Stickley. You must not consider me a champion of this race of which I am, perhaps, not fully advised. Since I have been here I visited on one occasion a court of law, and the proceedings I observed might account for the condition cited in your opening remarks. Be that as it may, I would regard it

THE GOVERNOR'S OPINION

as a precautionary measure to crush out this all too prevalent practice of dispensing law by individual citizens; for it must eventually destroy respect for the legally constituted authority."

"Of course," said the Governor thoughtfully, "a state cannot always prevent a demonstration on the part of its citizens, particularly in the case of certain crimes."

"Certainly," assented Mr. Bleecker; "but it seems to me that there is no crime too bad to be handled by law."

"Well, there is a large and influential majority in Magnolia that disagrees with that proposition. And who knows but what the majority is right?"

Mr. Bleecker was curious to know how His Excellency stood on the subject, yet he feared to ask any direct question in the face of his wife's look of reprimand. He did, however, venture interrogatively:

"But, personally —?"

"Personally, I would close up the business of the State any day to go out and help lynch a nigger."

The reply astounded even the most radical of the guests, and Morris Bleecker chided himself for his curiosity. Some of the ladies present coughed and squirmed uneasily, while others looked at the Governor with a stare of uncomprehending wonder, and Jack Carter, the reporter for the Savna *Times,* who was one of the guests, immediately got busy with his pencil.

For some time Uncle Abe had been standing in the dining-room door trying to catch his mistress' eye. Suddenly some one behind him touched him on the arm urgingly, and he entered and laid an open sheet of paper beside Mr. Bleecker.

For a moment the host was disconcerted, and his

eyes passed quickly over the words before him; then he read out loud:

"'A delegation of Negroes to see the Governor. It is a case of life and death.'"

At this juncture it is necessary to return to Elsa, who had been left by Allan at the house of the minister, Brother Stevens.

She and the minister's wife had been quietly talking, while the divine was in the adjoining study; and they were beginning to think of retiring, when the doorbell sounded. Mrs. Stevens, who answered the call, was greatly shocked by the unceremonious entrance of a half-dozen officers, a few of whom were in uniform. Babe Ellis was in the lead and acted as spokesman.

"We want this yaller wench heah. And where's the buck gone?" he inquired in typically Southern accents.

Hearing the commotion, the Reverend Mr. Stevens quickly entered and asked what might be the matter.

"Matter enough," echoed Babe Ellis. "Some of your gang of niggahs have killed a white man. Where's that fellah Allan?" he asked, with a searching glance about the room.

The minister informed the man that he did not know; then, catching sight of Elsa in charge of an officer, he nervously enquired what they were going to do with her.

"Put her in jail," was the unfeeling answer.

"Could you not leave her in our care? We will be responsible for her appearance at any proceedings, or we will give whatever bond you may require," pleaded the minister.

In an official tone Babe answered:

" Would be glad to accommodate you, but in such cases bail is seldom evah given."

The minister's wife added her entreaties to those of her husband, and they gave Babe the names of many influential persons of his own race who would vouch for the girl, even going so far as to offer cash security to a large amount; but all such proposals were rejected by the officer.

Suddenly the mellow notes from a trailing-hound's throat rang out upon the air, and as the sound died away there arose the answering call of many others.

" That's Nero. He's struck a trail! " cried Babe excitedly. " Heah, two uv you fellahs take the gal to the station, and the rest uv you follow me."

And he departed in pursuit of his quarry, closely followed by his comrades.

Elsa, accompanied by Mrs. Stevens, left with the two officers, while Brother Stevens went to the nearest telegraph station to advise the Bishop,— who was nearly a day's journey away, in pursuit of his duties,— of the mischance that had befallen his daughter. After having done that, he called up the District Attorney by telephone, in an effort to arrange bond; but this official, because of the lateness of the hour, was uncommunicative.

In passing down a side street on which were located a number of saloons the pastor heard a voice haranguing the inmates. Curiosity prompted the good man to listen; and from what he could glean he came to the conclusion that it was the man who had retreated so ingloriously from the encounter with Allan at the Bishop's house. With whiskey and hatred the man was inflaming the minds of his bibulous brethren, while he filled their ears with a tale of how " a whole passel uv niggahs" had jumped on him and his partner, that they had killed his partner, and that he had had to run for his life.

Knowing that this tale would be carried from one resort to the other, Brother Stevens determined to act quickly, for there was no doubt that soon there would be a howling, cursing multitude crying for vengeance, and he shuddered to think what might happen. Remembering that Allan had spoken of the Governor's being a guest of Mr. Bleecker in the mansion on the shell-road, he repaired to the home of one of his colleagues, and by messenger and telephone the two soon had summoned a delegation and were on their way to call on the Governor.

Meanwhile Henry Sage, a friend whom Allan had had placed at the head of one of the branches of the Union of Ethiopia, had learned of the difficulty and, by means of a signal previously agreed upon, was gathering a number of adherents for mutual defense.

The delegation had now arrived at the Bleecker house and had sent in a request to see the Governor. He, much to the surprise of the assembled guests,— after his radical remarks,— graciously consented to receive his ebon callers, who were soon informed that His Excellency was awaiting them in an anteroom.

" Well, what can I do for you?" was the Governor's condescending question, uttered in the most supercilious tone.

The Reverend Mr. Stevens, who was spokesman, proceeded to relate rapidly and convincingly the events of the evening, describing in detail the encounter of Allan, the causes leading to it, and the additional fact, which he had further learned, that the man in question was not dead, but that he had an even chance to recover.

"As we left the city, a large mob was gathering with the express purpose of storming the jail; and as they have refused to accept bond for our Bishop's daughter, we dread to think what might happen," concluded the minister in a hopeless tone.

"But cannot the sheriff handle the situation?" queried the Governor.

"The sheriff has joined the chase for Allan, and there are only two minor officers on guard," was the reply.

"One moment," said the Governor; and he left the room to go to the telephone in a nearby apartment. There he remained closeted for a short while, during which he was in communication with the sheriff's wife. She was fully informed as to the whole affair and confirmed the report that a mob was forming, that the guard at the jail was inadequate, and added the information that there was only one negro prisoner besides the Bishop's daughter. On the Governor's asking her if she feared for her own safety, she assured him that she felt herself to be in no danger, but thought that the negro prisoners might suffer.

The Governor returned to the delegation and told them that he would take the matter under advisement, an announcement that filled them with a depression they could not conceal. Feeling it useless to continue the interview longer, they were preparing to depart, and the Governor was about to return to the festal board, when the 'phone again rang.

"Is that the Governor?" came the voice of the sheriff's wife.

Then she went on to tell him that large groups of

armed negroes were congregating at a certain point in the city, with the evident purpose of opposing the mob. The Governor, at the information, hurriedly called up an adjutant and told him of the situation.

" How soon can you have a detachment of the Savna Guards on the scene? " he asked.

" In twenty minutes," was the reply.

" Very well," returned the Governor; " you can take care of the situation. Remember, the blacks are armed," he cautioned.

" Trust me, Governor; I'll attend to that "— with equal significance.

Returning to the delegation in the next room, the Governor informed them that the troops had been ordered out, whereupon, thanking him for the step he had taken to prevent trouble, the black callers passed from the gubernatorial presence.

CHAPTER XI

PANDEMONIUM

True to his promise, the military official had summoned a troop of thirty men, and they made their way immediately toward the scene of the trouble.

The troops were marching down the street that led diagonally to the jail when they encountered a nondescript array of cursing, vociferating human beings carrying weapons of all sorts, while looming above the crowd was a stalwart son of Magnolia bearing a coil of rope. This seething mass of humanity was constantly being augmented by men of every grade of life,— the rich and the poor, the high and the low, the seer and the sage, the youth and the simpleton, the thoughtful and the thoughtless, the vicious and the violent, the chattering ape and the surly bear, the grinning monkey and the awkward kangaroo, the ghoulish hyena and the skulking panther, the lion in his fury and the man-eating tiger, the vulture and the vampire, the deadly cobra and the cowardly jackal, the brute and the human, the man and the beast, the sycophant and the senile, the brave and fair and the hideous and homely; the descendant of the courtier and the offspring of the ticket-o'-leave man, the blue blood of Magnolia and the scum of the swamp lands, the plowman and the poet, the clerk and the cart-driver, the drug fiend and the rounder, the gourmand and the

77

gambler, the tin-horn and the blackleg, the tout and the snitch, the licentious and the lewd, the proud, the haughty, the princely, and the cringing and cowardly, the night-rider and the Ku-Klux, the redshirt ruffian and the midnight assassin, the hero of the Lost Cause and the ex-dealer in human flesh, the smouldering vengeance of the former master and the carking hate of the ex-slavedriver, the villainous Legree and the scheming Marks,— every one of the Caucasian type, with the strain of many nationalities.

This was the Southern mob: an institution confined not wholly,— though largely,— to Magnolia, but peculiar to Unionland as a whole. These men were out for a lark, they were about to indulge in a favorite diversion,— a diversion far more popular than the tango dance, far more interesting than the latest opera. Here was a diversion that furnished amusement as well as satiated their lust for blood; while the victims were an inconsequential factor of society.

Under the full glare of the electric lights the small military detachment swung jauntily into the Avenue of the Bastille. Some of the members of the mob greeted these fellow-townsmen with friendly remarks. The leading column of the troops had involuntarily executed a movement in the direction of the jail, when the harsh command rang out:

" Forward! March! "

And the men in uniform proceeded to a different quarter of the city, while the mob serenely went its way. There seemed to be no uncertainty as to the destination of the uniformed band, for it advanced steadily until it reached a humble section of the city and drew up before a rather pretentious hall. Luke Dean, who had been found a ready tool with which to destroy the plans of self-protection arranged for his people, had divulged the rendezvous of the black defenders of the cause.

Inside the hall were about eighteen Ethiops drilling under command of Henry Sage, Allan's friend. The door of the hall being unfastened, the commander of the thirty militiamen filed into the place, followed by his troop. Facing the startled defenders, he exclaimed in a commanding tone:

" In the name of the law I command you to surrender your arms!"

A tragic silence prevailed for a moment; then Henry Sage stepped forward and addressed the officer in command.

" If you please, sir," he began, " we wish to assist you in preserv —"

" I will have none of your clatter. Lay your arms in the middle of the floor," interrupted the officer warmly.

" But I hope you will hear me," said Henry, with polite insistence. " You know there is a large mob gathering —"

But he got no further.

" I command you for the third and last time to do as I have ordered," said the officer sternly.

It was a tense moment, and a breathless silence pervaded the hall. Henry Sage was the pivot on which the whole situation moved and he was to prove himself equal to the occasion. Walking up to within arm's reach of the commandant and meeting him squarely, eye to eye, Henry raised his arm in an impressive manner and said:

" If not in the name of the law, then in the name of Justice you *will* hear me."

The officer, white with rage, turned and gave the command:

"Ready! Load! Aim!"

But simultaneously Henry had given the same command to his little corps, and when the officer turned to face his enemy before giving the command to fire, he found himself looking into the barrels of eighteen rifles. The sight brought him to his senses, for in the swarthy faces before him he could see a deadly determination to back up their leader.

A lieutenant stepped forward now and whispered something in his captain's ear. That officer nodded, then in a surly tone asked:

"Well, what do you want to say?"

"That's better," remarked Henry. Then, going on: "It was at the request of my people that troops were ordered out. We had hoped that you would disperse a mob that is approaching the jail, in which an estimable lady of our race has been placed. You may imagine our surprise when your command came here, as we are in no sense in a condition of riot. We have congregated our little band so that in the event of failure to secure troops we would protect her at all hazards. Now, sir, we are willing to obey the laws of the state, but even while we are conversing a bloodthirsty mob is battering at the jail-door for admission. Under these conditions, do you think it a reasonable thing that we should question your motives?"

The officer winced at the clear-cut language and the sincere tone in which the words were uttered; he could not meet the other's honest gaze fairly, and his answer was an evasion.

"These are matters for the state to take care of," he said, concluding with the words: "You said you

were willing to obey the law; then, deliver your guns
as you were ordered to do."

"We must first have assurances that you will disperse the mob if we comply."

"Are we not the constituted authority of the state,—
bound by our oath to preserve the law?" asked the
officer.

"We do not question your authority," returned
Henry; "but because you have passed by these rioters
and have sought us out, we feel that we have reason to
doubt the sincerity of your motives. But, if you will
promise us on your word as a gentleman that you will
proceed immediately and disperse the mob, we will deliver our weapons."

"I will do nothing of the kind," the other snapped
viciously.

"Then, neither will we surrender our arms." And
the light of battle shone again in the eyes of the dusky
civilians.

Another parley now ensued between the captain and
his second in command, after which the superior officer,
turning to Henry, said:

"Very well; I promise."

"On your honor as a gentleman of Magnolia,"
asked Henry, as if he were administering an oath.

"On my honor as a gentleman of Magnolia," repeated the other firmly.

"Do you agree?" asked Henry, turning to his fol-
lowers.

"Yes; we agree," came the assenting chorus.

And marching forward, the small body of blacks
deposited their arms, with a clatter, in a heap before
their former opponents.

No sooner had this act been performed than an

Ethiop youth, hatless and panting with excitement, rushed into the hall, yelling:

" Quick! quick! They have broken into the jail and are killing everybody in it! "

The unarmed black band looked expectantly at the commander of the white corps. And quickly enough did that captain speak.

" Arrest that man," he ordered, indicating Henry Sage; " and the balance of you go and search the nigger quarters for arms."

The ebon defendants, recognizing the futility of dealing with such antagonists, departed almost in a body, while, without a word of protest, Henry submitted to arrest.

The report that the mob had broken into the jail was only too true. The battering down of the heavy doors of the prison had taken nearly a half-hour, during which time the petty officers in charge had made no effort at defense. Once these barriers were down, the mob swarmed through the corridors, peering into the cells for a victim. They did not succeed in discovering Elsa, for the sheriff's wife had taken her and Mrs. Stevens into her own apartments. An aged Ethiop cowered in the farthest corner of one of the cells.

" Here's one, boys! " some one shouted, poking a dim lantern close to the protecting bars.

Instantly the crack of a dozen rifles rang out, and the poor old man sank weltering in his own blood. He had gone to his last accounting.

The sound of shooting caused an involuntary shudder to run through the little band of women in the sheriff's apartments. Mrs. Stevens was softly weeping, while Elsa was kneeling beside her, bravely assuring her that she felt no fears for her safety. Nor had the sheriff's wife any doubt as to the security of her female prisoner, for whom she had formed a genuine liking during their short time of association. She was particularly attracted by the girl's polished manner, by her obvious culture and refinement.

Suddenly the telephone rang in an adjoining room, and the sheriff's wife went to answer the call, leaving Elsa and Mrs. Stevens alone conversing. Through Elsa's mind was passing the thought that perhaps they had taken Allan prisoner; but her perturbation of mind on his account did not show itself in her manner.

Mrs. Stevens, who had persistently refused to leave Elsa, despite the girl's protest at her sacrifice, had just said:

"Your father will be here by noon. It is now three o'clock in the morning. But perhaps the brothers will have us out by the time he comes."

And Elsa, who was not thinking of herself, had replied:

"We can't ever say that we've never been in jail."

And at that very moment a heavy knock sounded on the door, which was immediately opened, and a head covered with a sombrero was thrust in, while a thick tongue enquired:

"Whah's the gal? Oh, here she is!"

And a man opened wide the door and strode into the room, saying:

"Come on, fellahs!"

The sound of many feet was heard in the corridor, and soon a number of his companions entered the room. At the sight of them Mrs. Stevens screamed and fell fainting on the floor.

Elsa had risen to her feet; calmly she folded her

arms and gazed at her tormentors,— her eyes were steady, unflinching.

The big leader of the brutes cowered in the face of the indomitable look, in which was written the very essence of the scene. Here was virtue arrayed against vice; purity against foulness; justice and right against lust and license; the scorn with which honesty and truth hurl back dishonesty and lasciviousness; the power unseen, by which the fearless man drives back the tiger cowering into the jungle.

The sheriff's wife, hearing the disturbance, rushed toward the scene, and drawing a revolver, she discharged it aimlessly. She was quickly disarmed, but this counter incident served to break the spell of the unseen protection that had up to this moment spared Elsa. The unfeeling mob surged forward, and laid their brutal hands upon the helpless girl.

Let us draw a veil over this sad and terrible scene.

They lynched her!

Do you say: Impossible!

I tell you: No!

This is no fantastic tale of the black death of a Peruvian princess; nor the story of the sacrificial victim of some pagan religious rite. This is not the account of the deeds of a Blue Beard, or of a Prince of Bagdad, or of some jealous Persian monarch. It is but the simple record of a day's happenings, displayed on the front page of one of the modern newspapers of Unionland.

Certain reformers indulge in heroics over what they term the White Slave Traffic;— frequently but the dereliction of some wilful, pampered miss, to whom no privilege is denied. And no doubt reform in that direction is much needed. But the white slave's fate and steps to its betterment assume an awkward, ungainly stride, marked with the limp of insincerity, when contrasted with the barbarous performance,— such as herein recorded,— in which her sister of the darker hue is the victim, and concerning the truth of which an oppressive silence is maintained. But let us leave the question of national retributive justice to a higher power and content ourselves with the simple inscription here of these events.

The morning dawned bright and clear. It was the Sabbath. There seemed, however, to be no thought of worship in the being of the denizens of Savna. The mob of the early morning had increased to an immense concourse, and this mass had divided itself into four or five separate bodies, all obsessed with the one idea,— to kill. It had grown into an army of homicidal monomaniacs unloosed upon a defenseless people. Occasionally the Sabbath air would be filled with the sound of cheering and ghastly laughter when some particularly brutal act was perpetrated against some unoffending and unprotected Ethiop.

As the morning grew, the mobs covered all portions of the city, burning and pillaging the residences of the helpless defenders. Inconceivable acts were committed. An aged, tottering Ethiop had just alighted from a street car; they pounced upon him with clubs and stones and left him lifeless beside the curbing. A number of Ethiops had gathered in a church, secure in the protection of its sanctity, they thought. They were engaged in singing hymns and making prayers when the place that should have given them sanctuary was invaded by the demoniacs; the singing was changed to the moans of the injured, the prayers, to the groans of the dying. Near the wharf a cabin had been set in flames. A young Ethiop mother dashed within its single entrance to rescue her babe that had been left inside. The mob rolled a bale of cotton against the one opening, and the mother and child perished.

A young Ethiop driving an automobile was hauled from his car and beaten to death with clubs. It was Luke Dean, whom retributive justice had thus quickly overtaken. He had met the reward of his own duplicity.

It would be sad indeed to indite the full account of the many heartrending and pitiless acts of cruelty in this saturnalia of crime; it is sufficient to tell that the black victims were numbered by the hundreds ere the fury of the mob was spent. Former neighbors of the opposing races became enemies in a moment and strove to wreak the vengeance of Cain upon one another. The smouldering hatred of centuries seemed to have been crystallized into one day's performance. The centuries had turned back on their hinges and had revealed not a Christian country but a land revelling in the savage orgies that abounded in medieval days.

At midday a man, bearing a small black handbag, alighted from a train at the Savna station and was preparing to make his way toward the city. The station master pleaded with him not to go, telling him of the conditions existing there; but his account simply served to accelerate the traveler's movements, and he strode hurriedly toward the environs of the city. It was Bishop Mangus.

Quickly the Bishop made his way toward his home in the suburbs. The sight that met his gaze at every turn was appalling; on every hand the ruin and desolation of his parishioners was apparent; yet he pressed steadily on, undaunted. On passing by the residence of Brother Stevens, whom he had appointed to his pastorate in this, his home town, the Bishop paused. All that was left of the once attractive cottage were a few charred and smoking remains. Curiously the Bishop stepped among the ruins, and as he did so, his foot struck something round and hard. It was a human skull,— all that remained of poor Aunt Jane. But the Bishop did not know.

Resuming his way, he passed by the armory where the colored troops had held their meetings. Another dead body lay in his path, face downward. The Bishop stooped and turned the face of the dead man toward him. He found himself looking upon the features of Henry Sage, whose body had been pierced in a dozen places. A tear fell from the eye of the living as he looked on the dead. He had known and loved this brave young man.

Continuing his painful progress, the Bishop soon arrived at his own premises. He was more than half prepared for the scene that met his eyes. As he had anticipated, it, too, was in ashes. Leaning his arms on the gate-post, with his head buried in his hands, he gave himself up to sad reverie. He wondered what his little girl would say when she learned of the destruction of their home. No doubt she was safe among some of his people. While he stood thus lost to the present, an ominous noise of distant shouting and cursing became audible,— a noise that seemed to grow ever nearer; but the Bishop heeded it not.

A white neighbor passing by laid a kindly hand on the black man's shoulder and said:

"I know it's hard to lose our family; but come with me. See,— the mob is approaching! And you may lose your own life as well."

" 'Lose our family?' " repeated the Bishop. " What do you mean? " he shouted in the tones of one awakened from a dream and with a look of ferocity such as never yet emanated from mortal eye.

His informant shrank back in awe; but seeing the threatening mob advancing, he pulled at his companion's sleeve to urge him away, answering at the same time:

" Did you not know that they had hanged your daughter? "

" Hanged my daughter? " repeated the father in a dazed, mechanical fashion, as if he had not quite understood.

" Yes," said the neighbor, deeply touched at the poignant grief of the man before him. " And you must hurry, or they will kill you, too."

But the Bishop did not even hear. They had hanged his little Elsa,— his joy, his life.

" Come! " urged the neighbor in a final appeal; for the mob was upon them now.

" No! " cried the bereaved man, covering his face with his hands. " Now let me die, too."

The mob was only too willing to accommodate him, and soon his bruised and battered form was lying prostrate upon the pavement.

The evening dew was falling when the Bishop, who had been left for dead, regained consciousness and began to wander aimlessly about. He could not think; all within him was confusion. Mechanically he made his way to the railroad yards, where a kindly hand was laid upon his arm and he was led into a car that was standing on a siding.

It was Jacob Whiteside, who was waiting with his car for a party of tourists.

After a night's rest the Bishop awoke refreshed, yet still terribly sore. Even in the morning light he was not quite sure that it had not all been a dream. Therefore, the first question he asked of Whiteside was:

" Is it true about — about —" He could get no further.

But Whiteside understood and mournfully assured him that it was.

A tense silence followed; then at length Bishop Mangus found his voice.

" Now," he cried, " you may count on me as a full-fledged member of the Union of Ethiopia."

CHAPTER XII

PEONAGE

It seems an imposition to treat the reader to so continuous a succession of horrors; but it is necessary, since this narrative is intended to portray a phase of life that is all too prevalent in Unionland,— a phase concerning which the public conscience needs to be awakened. I wish that it were possible to class as an anachronism the occurrence of these horrors in a civilized country. And just so surely as the public begins to view these performances through unprejudiced eyes will there be so universal condemnation of the mob spirit that its rule will cease.

Let us now take up the chase of Allan Dune on his flight from the mansion on the shell-road. Allan's acquaintance with the surrounding country was slight, but he took his course in a northerly direction, skirted the city, and headed for the thickly wooded country. He could hear the baying of the hounds, and he could not help wondering how often the drama in which he was an actor had been presented in this very region. His pursuers were following his trail with dogged persistence, and he knew that they would eventually overtake him, unless some fortunate circumstance intervened. Then through his mind flashed old stories that his father used to tell him of how he threw the hounds off his trail; and, coming to a small stream, Allan, instead of crossing, walked along its course in the shallow water for some miles; then he continued northward. He had evidently succeeded in eluding his pursuers; at least temporarily. He could see in the east streaks of light that indicated the approach of daylight, so he thought it wise to seek some place of concealment.

Allan was now passing down a lane on each side of which were farms of the people of his own race. Some of the houses were pretentious, and the fields about showed careful cultivation,— a fact that seemed to disprove the theory of a lack of initiative on the part of the freedman when working for himself. The country itself was picturesquely beautiful, abounding in squirrels and many varieties of feathered creatures. Allan delighted in this communion with nature, where the different species of animal life mingled so harmoniously. Then to him occurred the thought of his pursuers; and all at once it seemed that they were some carniverous creature scenting out him, the prey.

The sun by this time had risen, and Allan, feeling the pangs of hunger, stopped at a humble cottage where he had caught sight of a middle-aged woman of his own race. She greeted him with the hospitality for which Magnolia is noted and invited him to enter. She was preparing breakfast when her guest entered, and her son (she was a widow) was busy harnessing a team preparatory to driving to town.

In a short time the meal was ready, and all sat down to eat. The young son,— he was about twenty,— had been talking with someone in the city by 'phone, and he had learned some meager details of the work of the mob. On Allan's questioning him closely, the young man imparted the information that some one had been lynched in the city, but nothing definite was to be learned. Allan was pressing him for some further details when the ominous notes of the bloodhounds sounded on his ear.

Hastily pressing a gold piece upon his startled hostess, Allan darted out of the rear door, leaving her exclaiming:

"Oh, Lawdy! What's the matter?"

This farm at which Allan had stopped was about twenty miles from the city of Savna. A railroad ran at about a mile's distance from the house. With unabated vigor the hounded man sped toward the track. The dogs now saw their quarry, and so did their masters, who were on horseback; and they redoubled their efforts to overtake their prey. A number of ineffective shots were fired, but though the lead failed to reach him, the dogs were steadily gaining.

A freight train was just getting under headway, but Allan feared that by the time he should reach the tracks its speed would be too great for what he was trying to compass. He was now about one hundred yards from the track, and the lead hound was about the same distance from him. The dog had ceased baying and was racing silently forward to attack its certain prey, when Allan, with an energy born of desperation, leaped into the doorway of an open box-car. His legs protruded; but he clung to the side of the door with a grip of iron. The dog had followed so closely that it caught one leg of his trousers, tugging at it so savagely that it had almost pulled him back, when someone inside seized Allan by the wrists and pulled him into the car, saying:

"Come in, me bye; make yersilf at home."

It was Paddy the Bum. He had witnessed the race

with great enthusiasm and with the eye of a true sportsman. The dog, finding itself baffled, with almost human emotion, growled angrily at the retreating train.

"Lonesome Bill here and I jist bet a can on ye, an' I win me bet," continued Paddy.

"But if ye hadn't give him a lift ye'd a lost," commented Lonesome Bill dryly. "Come, cheer up, me bye, we're not so particular because yer front is a little pillaged. Iverybody can't sport the glad rags like muh." And he plumed himself airily in his grotesque habiliments, as he gazed kindly at Allan, whose clothes were torn and hung in shreds, and who was hatless as well.

"Oh, I'm not concerned about my clothes," returned Allan. "My only regret is that I haven't my card with me."

"Pretty good!" exclaimed Paddy, his eyes a-twinkle. "But, you see, we are slumming and we're trying to fergit our sassiety manners. But may I enquire what was the cause of your abrupt *entrée?*"

Allan explained as much as he wished them to know and thanked Paddy heartily for his assistance.

"Arrah, me bye, don't mintion it. I've got a string of hero medals, an' loife-savin' is an everyday occurrence with me. But have ye got a bit o' terbaccy about yez?"

He and lonesome Bill were smoking the snipes of cigars, which were very short.

"Oh, throw those things away," said Allan, putting his hand to his vest pocket as if he were going to pull forth some fresh ones.

Instantly the men tossed the butts away.

"That's right," approved Allan, retreating to the

end of the car. "I never encourage the use of tobacco."

Paddy and his partner looked back ruefully in the
direction in which their lost stubs had disappeared,
then they started after Allan, crying:

"Let's toss him overboard."

But when they got within an arm's length of Allan
he slipped his fingers in his vest pocket and drew forth
a shining gold coin, which he quietly deposited in
Paddy's outstretched hand. Paddy looked at the
money in amazement.

"Tin dollars!" he ejaculated, while visions of
copious schooners and untold free lunches flitted
through his mind. "But ye're rale shure it ain't
tainted money?" he questioned cautiously, pretend-
ing to hesitate about receiving it; while Lonesome Bill
stood carefully near, so as to insure the retention of
the money in case Paddy had really lost his senses.

"Don't give yourself any uneasiness on that score,
my friend; I am now no longer connected with the
trust," laughed Allan.

"Oh, then; under them circumstances Oi'll take it.
But ye see, Oi was afraid ye moight raise the price of
some commodity; an' Oi couldn't bear to see the poor
public suffer from yure ginerosity."

Imbued with the spirit of the jolly, devil-may-care
"life on the road," they were holding high carnival
when the train slowed down at Bale's Siding,— a telegraph stationed named after the owner of the nearby
plantation.

Cale Bale, his son George, and an Ethiop past sixty
were walking down the length of the train, peering into
each car. Each one of the trio carried a rifle. When
they reached the car where Allan and his companions

of the road were, they leveled their weapons at them,
and Bale ordered:

" All hands out! "

Allan and his fellow-travelers alighted.

" I'm justice of the peace here," announced Bale;
" and you may consider yourselves under arrest."

" An' fer what? " asked Paddy.

" For bumming," was the response.

" Shure, an' there must be some mistake. Me friend
and Oi have been travelin' in me private car here, an'
the naygur is me valet."

" It's a swell car," said Bale, amused in spite of himself. " I 'spose your friend is president of the road? "

" Shure, an' yure wrong again," said the loquacious
Paddy. " We're both retired capitalists, an' we have
an appointment to dine at the Commercial Club at
Louisburg this very noight."

" Well, we don't want you two anyway," returned
Bale, with a leer that took the place of a laugh. " It's
your valet we want."

" Raley, we can't spare him, yer hanner. He's a
very valuable man, an' takes all the worry an' details
of trav'lin' off our moinds." Paddy waxed eloquent
in his effort to gain Allan's release, but all his wit and
pleading availed nothing.

It was the busy season of the year, Bale needed
hands badly, and it was by this method that he secured
them. Allan, knowing that it was useless to parley
with him, accompanied the trio to the big house nearby,
in one corner of which the magistrate had his office.

As soon as they had entered the office, Bale sat down
in his chair and took from the top of the desk a statute
book, from which he read aloud a pargraph; then, looking at Allan, he said:

"Guilty, or not guilty?"

"Oh, just suit yourself," answered Allan with a wave of his hand.

"Guilty," answered Bale, writing in a book as he spoke. "Six months." Then turning to the old Ethiop, who had remained close to him, he went on: "His number is 35, Bill. Put him to work in the blue ridge field."

"Yes, sah," answered that dignitary; and he and his charge departed together.

On the way to the field Allan tried to sound his companion, who, however, proved stiff and uncommunicative. Though Allan plied the old man with questions as to how long he had been in his present position, what pay he received, and so on, the old darkey refused to reply. Allan began to wonder how he could interest him. He was due in Cargo City in five days, and he felt it imperative that he should escape.

As he and his guard were passing a gang of laborers, some of whom were women, — and who had all been surreptitiously obtained from both the city and the countryside by false charges of various misdemeanors, the charge constituting their sole offense, — a young woman, weak and sickly in appearance, lagged behind her fellow laborers, though it was plain that she was doing her best. At the sight of this Bill stopped, and walking over to the young woman, he dealt her a stinging blow with the butt of a whip he carried.

It was the repetition of scenes enacted nearly a half-century previous, — it was the peonage system, which flourishes even to-day to a large degree in Magnolia land. In order to render himself immune from this corporal punishment, Allan knew that it was necessary to do something quite out of the ordinary. Walking over to the old man, who had been a slave driver, he said in a tone of cool menace:

"Any man that will strike a woman of his race in such a manner is less than a cur."

"Oh, never min'; we'll 'tend to you," was Bill's retort.

"Yes; and you will find that I will require your attention," said Allan pointedly feeling that the man's enmity was better than his former attitude of cold disdain.

Nothing more transpired between them until they reached their destination, when Bill directed Allan to the digging of some post holes. There was three hours' work before sunset; and, while Allan worked faithfully, his wits were never idle. There were numerous guards, and he realized the futility of attempting to escape by open flight.

At length the supper bell rang, and, together with the other laborers, Allan made his way to a group of cabins not far from the residence of the owner. Among the motley crowd that wended its way homeward were all sorts of offenders, from those whose misdemeanors were of the most trivial character, — such as being "sassy and impudent" — to those whose peccadillos were of a more serious character. One of those guilty of the former offense was an Ethiop boy of seven years.

Allan pushed his way forward until he had reached the side of Bill, who preceded the throng. After a few preliminary remarks, he painted to the old slave-driver in glowing colors the wonderful achievements of his people; how they had built up large and thriving institutions of learning, how they had established communities of their own,— and by way of example, he cited a famous educational institution not far from their present abode. He told the old man of the professional men of his race, of their journals, their theaters, their commercial enterprises, and their manufacturing interests in various parts of Unionland. But, though Allan waxed eloquent over his theme, Bill remained taciturn and refused to be drawn out.

At length Allan brought the matter to a direct, personal application.

" There is no reason," he said with conviction, " why you shouldn't have a plantation of your own, like this one, and live in as good a house as Cale Bale."

It was a bold move, but Allan could see that it had produced effect; for in the gathering dusk he remarked that old Bill's face lighted up, and the man half turned his head, as if he were going to answer him. This remark of Allan's had revived the one dream of the old man's life. He had worked year after year in the hope of earning sufficient money to purchase a farm of his own; and yet at the end of every year he would still be in debt to the store that Bale owned, although he would stint himself even to denying himself many of the necessities of life. After his annual accounting with Bale's bookkeeper he would go off and get drunk, then he would come to Bale himself in the big house. And the following conversation would always occur:

" Don't I make you my manager ? "

"Yea ; — but dat's all I gits out of it."

" Don't I pay you sixty dollars a month, which is more than any nigger in the state is getting ? "

"Yes ; but whar's de money ? "

" You'd ought to live within your means. You know I have always advised you to live within your means."

And then Bale would take down a big demijohn and pour a very large tumblerful of brandy for Bill and a small one for himself, and they would drink together. Then, after one more day of riotous living, Bill would return to his duties for another year.

But to resume: Allan had succeeded in interesting the old man, and he knew that he had made a valuable discovery. They had now reached the servants' quarters, and Bale was in the scale house as usual, waiting for Bill's daily report on the conduct of the employees. He still maintained a whipping-post, and one cabin with grated windows was used as a place of detention.

Bill, as was customary, to-night recounted the various acts of the laborers, some of whom he commended, others of whom he condemned to be whipped. When he came to Allan he said:

" Dis feller am dangerous. T'inks hisself as good as white folks."

" Oh, he does,— does he? " And Bale looked at Allan sternly. " Put him in the hold-over. I'll 'tend to him in the morning."

The other laborers were duly disposed of, and Allan was locked in the dreary, barred cabin. The stillness and solitude offered him opportunity for reverie. His mind went back to Savna. He wondered what had really occurred there, if his pursuers had really abandoned their chase, and if the mob had selected another victim on whom to vent their rage.

Strange thoughts filled Allan's mind in that lonely little cabin. He dwelt on Bunyan and on St. Paul, who escaped so miraculously; and he asked himself the question why such miracles could not be repeated to-day. He was a firm believer in the power of the Supreme Being to deliver him from any adverse condition. He knew himself to be the victim of an institution at which society winked; and suddenly he became doubly anxious to secure his release so that he might not fail to meet his colleagues in Cargo City on the date that had been set for the meeting of the convention.

It was nine o'clock at night, and Allan was beginning to feel the pangs of hunger when he heard a key being inserted in the door of his keep, and presently Bill entered carrying a pitcher of water and a big corn pone.

" Here's your supper," he grunted.

Allan thanked him profusely and invited him to sit on the rude bench that stood at one side of the room. Bill, however, ignored the invitation and, lantern in one hand, he held the door latch with the other and prepared to depart. Out of the corner of his eye Allan was watching the old man closely, but he said nothing. Bill hesitated on the threshold. Allan felt that all was not yet lost.

" Where'd you come from? " asked the old man suddenly. It was the first time he had shown any inclination to talk.

" Oh, I've traveled quite generally," answered Allan, jumping into the opening; " but more recently I have come from Savna. On my way here I have passed through a section that is undergoing a most remarkable change. Towns and villages of our people are springing up as if by magic. They have their own officials, and altogether govern themselves. They are doing an immense amount of business, and nearly all the trades and professions are represented. Their residences are of an excellent type, many of them being palatial in character, and their farms — "

"Well?" queried Bill as Allan paused.

"I observed a large number of small tracts of land, on which apparently are located a happy and contented people. I also saw a number of plantations that are owned by men of our race. You probably know Henry Margan, who lives fifteen miles below here."

Bill knew him, for he had regarded him with an envious eye for some years.

"Well, he owns twelve thousand acres,— all in a high state of cultivation; and when he started he was working at a much smaller salary than you are getting."

Allan had gleaned this information from a fellow laborer, but the other things he had mentioned he had actually observed.

"Yes, I know dat Mohgan; kain't read nor write no mo' den I kin."

"Certainly. He merely took advantage of his opportunities, exercised his rights as a man, never allowed anyone to hold him back and rob him of the thing rightfully due him."

Bill winced; he was becoming intensely interested.

"How much a yeah am sixty dollars a mont'?" he inquired.

Allan told him.

"An' fo' twenty-two yeah how much would dat be?"

"Fifteen thousand four hundred dollars," announced Allan.

Then Allan learned from the old man, as he talked further, that during the entire time that he had been with Bale he had spent only twenty-five dollars in actual cash, that he had lived very sparingly as to his personal apparel, and yet each year would find him in debt to the store.

There was a little more explanation, and then, as Bill was going he turned and asked once more:

"How much did yo' say dat was?"

"Fifteen thousand four hundred dollars."

"Fifteen thousand dollars," repeated Bill as he closed the door and secured it before departing to his own abode.

These figures kept recurring to Bill throughout the night, disturbing his customed peaceful slumbers. Toward morning he fell into a troubled sleep, and when he awoke, the sun was shining into his cabin window. He looked at his watch. It was nearly eight o'clock. During his entire twenty years' service this had never occurred before, except on the occasion of one of his annual sprees.

He dressed hurriedly and congregated his laborers in the mess shanty, where breakfast had long been prepared. Allan, watching the old man narrowly, saw that he was remote and *distrait*.

Bill did not partake of his breakfast, but instead made his way to the big house, where he never went except on such occasions as have been mentioned.

Bale had already breakfasted and was on his porch, preparatory to making his daily rounds, when up strode Bill. Bale, though surprised at this visit, spoke calmly, asking:

"Hullo, Bill. What's the matter."

"Nuffin'." Bill answered glumly.

It was evident to Bale that he was not drunk, and his manner was different from the air of petulant insolence displayed on former occasions.

"Everybody working?" ventured Bale.

" Nobody's wukin'," came the answer.

" What? " cried Bale, his wrath rising. " This cotton ready to go to waste, and nobody working! "

" I tells yuh jist whut, Mr. Bale,"— and he looked Bale squarely in the eye for the first time in his life — " I wants mah money."

" Oh, that's it," said Bale, who was beginning to feel a little uneasy. " Well, come into the office." And he led the way.

Bill followed silently. Bale took down his demijohn and glass and shoved them toward the old colored man. Then he got down a large account book from another shelf and began to busy himself with it, though all the time he was furtively watching his companion. Bill had refused to touch the liquor.

" How much do I owe you? " he queried, as a preliminary step.

" Fifteen thousand dollars."

Bale looked at the man in amazement. " You must be crazy! " he ejaculated, dropping his book.

" No, sah; dem figgers am right. I cal-lated Ise spent a few hundred dollars fo' close, an' de balance you owe me."

Bale wondered who could have been talking to Bill; and then he remembered having seen Allan gesticulating to him earnestly on the previous evening. He checked himself as he was on the point of asking about this newcomer, then said reassuringly:

" Come around this evening, Bill, and I'll have everything all fixed up."

" Oh, youse allus puttin' ut off like dat, Mr. Bale; but I wants mah money."

He had always addressed Bale as " Boss," and this new cognomen irritated his employer.

"Do you mean to say you doubt my word?" he blustered.

"I dunno nuttin' 'bout dat, but I wants mah money now."

Bale had been watching him, expecting the usual subsidence in his manner. But Bill was obdurate.

Bale now began to wheedle, trying to coax the darkey with flattering promises, but to no avail. At length, in a paroxysm of rage, he cried out:

"You black nigger, if you think I'm going to waste my time talking to you, you're mistaken! You're trying to place yourself on a level with white men."

Bill raised himself to his full height. For a moment he gazed calmly and unflinchingly at the man before him, and then, with a ring of pride in his voice, he said:

"Maybe I ain't as good at w'ite folks, but one t'ing I know, and dat is dat Ise a *man*."

This speech snapped the last thread of Bale's forbearance. Seizing a revolver that lay on his desk, he lifted it and fired it pointblank at Bill. The aged servitor fell, mortally wounded. A domestic, who had witnessed the scene, ran down to the mess-room of the waiting prison-laborers, telling them excitedly what had taken place. Confusion at once followed the announcement, and in the midst of it Allan Dune made his escape. By one of the freaks of fortune he secured passage on the same train that Jacob Whiteside was piloting, and on which was, too, the Bishop.

Cale Bale had the body of Bill removed and buried; but no thought of the killer's arrest and punishment even so much as entered the head of any of the authorities. The very suggestion of such action would have been derided by any resident of Magnolia.

CHAPTER XIII

THE DECEMVIRATE OF ETHIOPIA

Ephraim Johnston was a very busy man. He would have had no time to dream now, even had he so desired. His duties in connection with the Union furnished ample occupation.

The results of the initial convention of the Union of Ethiopia had far exceeded the wildest flights of imagination of the organizers. Their call for funds, sent out in accordance with their plans, had brought in so generous response that, to quote Eph, " the money rolled in by the cartload."

Eph, after having tried in vain to get in communication with the other members of the Union, was forced to use his own judgment in the conduct of affairs. In accordance with this, he had secured headquarters in a large office building up-town, and the click of typewriters, under the skillful manipulation of a half-dozen sets of nimble, dusky fingers of the female variety, could be heard all day long.

Eph had used the Cargo City National Bank as a depository for the funds of his society, and as his receipts had nearly reached the million-dollar mark, the recapitalization of the institution had been necessitated. Eph could not help smiling at the changed attitude of many of his former customers,— bankers, brokers, and men of that order,— who now treated him with studied respect; and he felt that perhaps he had fixed upon the solution of the race problem. Then he recalled the great masses of his people that were legislated against, and he knew that he must inevitably be classified among those thus publicly and legally ostracised.

The day for the second meeting of the Union of Ethiopia, which had been set for the fifth of October, had arrived, and Eph and his crew of assistants were filled with eager expectancy.

Allan, Bishop Mangus, and Whiteside, had, without further mishap, arrived on time.

Whiteside had imparted to Allan the news of Elsa's fate; and the only evidence of emotion that was perceptible was a firmer look of determination on his immobile face. Going over to the Bishop, whose hair had now turned white, he gently pressed the father's hand; and the Bishop knew that Allan knew and he burst into uncontrolled tears,— tears that Allan made no attempt to stay by words of consolation. He felt there was something holy about such grief. A bond of mutual sympathy had been established between these two, to which was added on the part of the younger man a sense of responsibility for his older associate.

In due time Chester A. Grant, the attorney, arrived, and after the most hearty greetings the four made their way to the new quarters, where Eph was awaiting them.

Allan assumed the gavel, and the Bishop, who acted as chaplain, delivered a most impressive and remarkable prayer,— one that revealed a marked freedom from his former conservative attitude. Reviewing at length certain unreconcilable distinctions of race and color, he prayed that the Father might remove the hampering cords of prejudice that bound the footsteps of his people at every turn and that excluded them from taking part in their own government. But the Bishop rose to the very heights of self-effacement when he prayed:

"If they still turn a deaf ear to our entreaties for justice and fair representation, in the words of the faithful patriarch, 'Let there be no strife, I pray thee, between me and thee, and between my herdmen and thy herdmen; for we be brothers.'"

He closed his prayer with a petition that the blessing of God might rest upon the Union and its purposes, and that its ends might be attained without friction.

The preliminary business of the meeting proceeded with dispatch until the point was reached when the call came for the reports of the progress made thus far by the organization, when the members were electrified by the completeness of the returns from the census they had inaugurated. A total count from every section of Unionland indicated an aggregate of fifteen million eight hundred thousand persons of Ethiopian descent or lineage. The census, which also recorded the literacy of black people, showed a ratio of seventy per cent. Many and varied were the comments indulged in at the revelation of these interesting facts; but it was only when Eph made his report on the moneys received,— which totaled $958,000,— that the stupendousness and the full seriousness of their undertaking began to dawn upon them. They then began to realize the extent of their responsibility. The report of the treasurer showed that the majority of the contributions had come in in sums of one dollar subscribed by each individual; a fact that indicated the enormous extent to which the race had been aroused as well as the popularity of the movement. In many instances the donors expressed a willingness to remit the same amount monthly.

The making of the reports ended, the convention went into secret session, from which, of course, the public was excluded. The proceedings, however, became common property in view of future developments. One of these was the establishment of the Bank of Ethiopia, with the members of the Union as its officers and directors.

A most important change in the personnel of the Union,— or, rather, an addition to it,— was proposed by Attorney Grant, who moved that each member name an associate, and that the organization should in future be known as The Decemvirate of Ethiopia; a motion that was adopted by all present.

It was further agreed that a substantial salary be paid to each member of the organization, who was to devote his entire time to the affairs of the society.

The introduction of new blood into the convention precipitated discussions of diverse character, which reopened the question of ultimate aims. Among the most persistent of the newcomers was Boyd Lindon,— a farmer who had been named by the Bishop as an associate,— who contended that there was no race question.

" I raise my hogs, my corn, my oats, and I sell them in the markets at the same price that my Caucasian neighbor gets. Why should I complain? " he asked.

"But have you no aspiration for something higher, no sympathy for those who have? " came the question.

"What's the use? When I see that I am not wanted elsewhere, and am being pushed by the law into some designated section, how can I change the course of affairs? " He looked about challengingly.

"You have almost answered your own question," replies Grant. "Perhaps it might be better if we were all farmers; but, unfortunately, we are not. And situated as we are,— that is to say, scattered over the length and breadth of Unionland,— we are, as you have intimated, pushed into the 'back seat' in the many activities in which we are engaged. We are supposed to accept conditions just as we find them. Then let our purpose be to try to correct them from this basis, rather than to assume something. If, as you have stated, we 'are not wanted,' does it not appear to be reasonable that we should agree to this wholesale segregation, that we should launch out in every line, without this hampering prejudice, into a community where there are no restrictions, either social or legislative, and where seventy per cent of its units have established their capability for self-government?"

Another new member,— a preacher, who had been named by Chester A. Grant,— addressed his associates in a voice full of deep emotion, saying:

"Gentlemen, it seems that you have not remembered that God has placed us here for some wise purpose,— that even our afflictions are by His will. We should consider the great religious forces that are at work trying to redeem mankind; we should think of the great and powerful denominations that are lifting up the Cross, and then we will stop and ponder on this mighty influence."

As the speaker paused, the Bishop, for the first time since the opening of the convention, rose slowly to his feet.

"I have been in the ministry," he began impressively, "for thirty-five years and, as you all know, have been an active leader in the church. I have preached

and prayed earnestly,— yea, fervently,— for the light,
for guidance; and now I can sum up my life experience
in a few words. I have done some good, I have
cheered some travelers; but if the church is to accom-
plish any substantial benefit to humanity, it must be by
means of a higher form of Christianity than that now
extant. I tell you plainly, gentlemen, that it is this
very division of sects and creeds that perpetuates the
feeling of prejudice and hatred between the races. It
was the church that supported unpaid servitude in ante-
bellum days, and to-day, as it now stands, it is a mute
champion of racial distinctions. But to reply more
pointedly to the good brother's remarks: If our afflictions are from God and for a wise purpose, then these
various denominations that are trying to aid us are
evidently working against God's will. But, of a truth,
my friends, when some religious truth is posited, by
which men shall receive some present, positive, and
actual reward in return to their obedience to the divine
demands, to the laws of equity, justice, and love for
our fellow-men, instead of the hazy and obscure promise of future world salvation; when the actual works
of the master Christian shall be here accomplished by
adherence to these pure motives and can only be
achieved by such purity, then the brotherhood of man
may become a reality among the possessors of such
religious truths; because there is a standard of ethics,—
of moral and spiritual rectitude,— to be attained that
completely annihilates the question of race or color."

The views of the Bishop were received with profound
respect, though with no little astonishment. But Allan
smiled in happy accord with the sentiments expressed.

The sessions of the Decemvirate were now held five

days each week, and the Bank of Ethiopia was doing a thriving business.

Thus a year went by, during which time the institution had established itself firmly in the commercial world. Contributions still kept coming in, and of the sixteen million Ethiopians in Unionland ten million were sending in at least one dollar annually.

Meanwhile the officers of the organization were negotiating for a strip of land lying south of the Ilo and east of the Isis rivers,— a tract that bordered on the sea coast. The governors of Unionland were kindly disposed toward the Decemvirate, although there was some opposition on the part of the residents of the section in which this strip of land was located; however, these residents were to be fully reimbursed for their holdings in the territory in question. As to this question of reimbursement, a discussion was precipitated in which Jacob Whiteside thus protested against such payment:

"My old father and mother,— and their ancestors before them,— paid for this land with their sweat and blood, their toil and privations, when, for centuries, they answered to the master's lash, reclaiming this territory from its primitive state and making it to blossom like the rose. To demand from us money for this land is practising usury with a vengeance. If individuals are to be held responsible for their misdeeds, why not nations? It is only an act of retributive justice that the territory should be ceded to the Decemvirate."

However, the cession could not be obtained, and Allan was appointed the envoy to conclude the purchase.

CHAPTER XIV

SOMETHING ABOUT RADIUM

Donald Bleecker,— nephew of the president of the Cargo City National Bank, cashier of the same institution, and, too, the gentleman with whom Allan had had an unpleasant encounter, as related in one of the opening chapters of this book,— was pacing up and down his narrow enclosure in the bank. He was troubled and appeared to be in the depths of thought. And so he was; for he had done a foolish thing and was fearful of the outcome of his mistake.

Donald was intensely interested in radium, and he had purchased a number of properties in a western province of Unionland that were reputed to be radium-bearing. A young friend of his,— a chemist who was studying at the Cargo City University,— was his most intimate associate, and together they had conducted experiments in Donald's quarters at the Bleecker mansion, a laboratory having been fitted up for the purpose.

A month previous to this day Donald had received a shipment of ores from his mines, and upon these ores he and the young chemist had been working assiduously. The scientist had found them rich in uranium and carnotite deposits, and the two men were jubilant. Having a perfectly appointed laboratory, they bent every effort toward the discovery of the perfect product. So far as they had gone they had been eminently successful; for they had found that every material object that gave off a reflection could be utilized and, when reduced in the crucible, aided materially in the production. Donald and his associate had maintained the utmost secrecy regarding their discoveries, although they might have sold their method for a substantial sum to the government,— but that sum would have been paltry compared with the project they had in view.

These two had been making experiments along various lines with the amount of the chemical that they had extracted, and some of the discoveries that had resulted filled them with astonishment as to the possibilities that might come of its use. They had produced photography through solid iron walls, and other results they had obtained had set Donald's thoughts working in a new direction. If, he reasoned, it were possible to produce photography through the attractive and cohesive properties of their output, what effect might it not have on gold? Nightly they had worked on their experiments in the direction that Donald had suggested, and at length their efforts met with success. Already they had made several practical demonstrations of their discovery, but the results of their nightly labors were known to them alone.

The Bank of Ethiopia having neither very secure nor commodious quarters, the directors had determined to let their millions lie in the vaults of the Cargo City Bank, which was burglar proof.

Now Donald and the chemist had constructed a peculiar contrivance, which the cashier had placed near the vaults and cleverly concealed with an unused overcoat. The two schemers had determined that the three days' exposure would be sufficient to compass their ends and they felt no uneasiness as to discovery or interruption, since these vaults were seldom used. There were still three days to wait, for they had only to-day placed the contrivance in position, but they had already engaged a private yacht to sail,— oh! they knew not where.

Mrs. Bleecker and her son Harold had been in Cargo City on a brief visit, but had returned to the shell-road mansion, consequently there was no one with Mr. Bleecker in the city house except Donald and the servants.

Allan, who now devoted his entire time to the business of the Decemvirate, was on the most friendly terms with his former employer. To-day he had called at the bank in regard to some important papers, and Mr. Bleecker had called Donald into his office to inquire about them, since they had been intrusted to the care of his nephew. Donald admitted having them, but he had left them at home, either in the library or in his laboratory.

Mr. Bleecker having an important engagement just then, and it being impossible for Donald to go at the moment, Allan, who needed the papers without delay, volunteered to go after them himself. Having been a former servant at the Bleeckers', he was accorded the freedom of the house.

Allan went to the Bleecker home, and after the maid had admitted him, he searched in the library for the papers that he wanted. His search there being unrewarded, he turned to seek his property in the laboratory. In handling the various papers in an effort to find his own, Allan came across dissertations on radium, unfamiliar text-books on chemistry, while his attention was held by an interesting article on pitchblendes. Then all at once he came across a drawing that would not have attracted his notice but for the fact that he saw the word "Gold," enclosed in a ring and indicating small objects, which was also followed by arrows that pointed to a strange-looking device. He soon came across the papers he wanted, and he was turning to leave the room when some strange prompting urged him to again examine the drawing that had aroused his interest.

Allan took the paper in his hand, and turning it over, found written transversely on it:

" It works, Bill! It works! "

He had known of Donald's companionship with the chemist, and he had no doubt but that the communication was meant for him. The words, however, for a moment puzzled him; then they seemed suddenly fraught with full meaning; and to his mind there came the thought of the millions of the Decemvirate that lay in the vaults of the Cargo City Bank. It all came to him with startling force. He felt that here was a matter that it would be worth while to investigate.

Without further reflection, he telephoned to Mr. Bleecker, requesting him to come home at once.

Donald, as soon as he had learned that Allan had gone to the Bleecker house in search of his papers, began to wonder if he had left anything of a suspicious nature on his desk at home; and as a consequence he was very uneasy. So, when the telephone rang, he picked up his own receiver, though the call was not for him, and he overheard Allan's request that his uncle should come home at once.

As soon as Mr. Bleecker had left the office, Donald donned his overcoat and hat, and hailing a taxicab, he followed his uncle's car at a distance and entered the house through a rear door at the very moment that Morris Bleecker went in at the front.

Allan, who had been eagerly awaiting Mr. Bleecker's coming drew the banker into the laboratory and hurriedly informed him of his fears and suspicions. At first Mr. Bleecker scoffed at the absurd idea that had entered Allan's head, but on being confronted with the drawing and all the other evidences of the alleged activity of this mineral, he began to regard the subject with rather more seriousness. On Allan's suggesting that they return to the bank and find out if there were any foundation for the fancy that had taken possession of him, Mr. Bleecker assented, and they prepared to depart. As they were going down the stairway the acute ears of the Ethiop heard the sound of footsteps retreating and then the slamming of the door of an unused exit.

Bidding Mr. Bleecker wait a moment, Allan hurried to the front door and saw the retreating form of Donald, who was just about to enter a taxi in waiting. In breathless haste Allan rushed back to the hall and urged Mr. Bleecker to hurry, at the same time acqainting him with what had occurred. In an instant they were in the banker's powerful car and were speeding on in a determined race for the bank, in violation of all the speed ordinances of the city, while a procession of motorcycle " cops " brought up the rear.

In the taxi ahead Donald was urging on his driver with curses and promises, while the big Bleecker car was swiftly and surely overhauling them. Allan, who was sure that the rascally cashier intended to destroy the incriminating mechanism, was determined that the true facts should be known. Being at the wheel of the car, he opened her up wide. The big machine fairly flew over the pavement, to the lasting delight of the newsboys and to the amazement of pedestrians.

It was a race never before witnessed on a crowded city thoroughfare, and the hairbreadth escapes and the thrilling near-accidents for which it was responsible would fill pages of a daily newspaper, yet it was over in nearly as little time as it has taken to tell it here. At the very last square Allan overhauled his adversary, and he and Mr. Bleecker had dismounted and were entering the building ere the taxi drew up.

Together Allan and the banker made a rapid survey of the scene, and Allan was in the act of lifting the concealing overcoat when Donald entered. His flushed face and angry scowl caused the eye of every clerk to be fixed upon him, and with wonderment they watched the scene. And when Allan picked up the device and quietly repaired with the president to Mr. Bleecker's private office, a look of such hate and baffled rage proceeded from the discomfited schemer that every one of the employees knew that something unusual was transpiring.

The evidence as to the intentions of the arch conspirator was all too unmistakable; but Allan and Mr. Bleecker exchanged no word of comment on the matter. The incident was closed.

After completing the business that had called him to the bank in the first instance, Allan left, and in passing out was forced to walk near the desk of Donald Bleecker. Without either looking up or addressing his remark to anyone, the cashier muttered in an undertone:

"I'll git you yet, Mr. Nigger."

Allan did not say anything in reply, but for the first

time in his life there fell upon him a nameless sense of
dread.

At the close of banking hours Mr. Bleecker called
his nephew into his office. What passed between them
will probably never be known, but some days later the
Cargo City *Chronicle* announced the retirement of Donald Bleecker from the position of cashier of the Cargo
City National bank, and added that he had retired to
his plantation in Magnolia.

Allan did not wish to act as the special envoy of the
Decemvirate on the mission for which he had been
chosen; but his knowledge of the affairs of the organization and the pressing appeals of its members made
it almost impossible for him to decline to serve. He
could not shake off a feeling of premonition, which
from time to time recurred to him; and sometimes it
seemed to him that the only thing to do would be to
refuse pointblank to go, despite the entreaties of his
confreres, the fear of being considered superstitious,
however, held him back.

His associates were somewhat taken aback when
Allan decided to make his will before starting out on
his mission. In this will he bequeathed all his pos-
sessions to a distant cousin whom he had never seen,—
his only living relative,— whose home was in Candia.
These personal arrangements attended to, Allan met
the Decemvirate in regular session and conferred with
them feelingly on the subject of his ambassadorship.
He reviewed at length the object of their union, re-
traced the history of its formation, and closed with the
impassioned appeal that they continue the work so
auspiciously begun.

"You have discussed in detail the various phases of
your tenure here in Unionland," he said in part, " and

as you are now agreed as to the irreconcilable barriers that separate you from the enjoyment of your social, civic, political and industrial rights, the only thing that can prevent the consummation of your object is weakness and lack of initiative of an original character on your part. You have won the sanction and approval of the government of Unionland, and if you now retrace your steps, I fear that you will find your position more serious and oppressive. If you will permit me to utter a prophecy, I would say that your present course will command and compel respect, will create in you a feeling of independence and patriotism, foster and encourage the establishment of business — and of enterprises of even a more extended nature — destroy that inherited feeling of the inferiority of your race and color, and restore the sovereign rights of man to each individual whom a prejudiced and contemptuous public has denuded of his birthright. You will, too, find yourselves enjoying untrammelled liberty and freedom. And now, my friends and brothers, if my mission should fail, I am leaving a complete record of all transactions, and you will have to send another representative to complete the negotiations. And now farewell."

The following day Allan Dune left for the city of Savna, in the province of Magnolia.

CHAPTER XV

A PYRAMID OF FIRE

Harold Bleecker, whom Allan had apprised of his intention to return to Savna, was in a state of pleased anticipation at the thought of the arrival of the friend of his invalid days. Harold, though able to walk now, was still a somewhat weak young man,— tall and pale and thin.

To-day he was waiting in his runabout for the coming of the Southbound train, which was to bring Allan Dune back to Magnolia. Soon the train pulled in at the Savna depot, and the scurrying passengers alighted, among them Allan, whose sharp eyes soon spied Harold. With hurried steps he sped to greet his former charge, his always friend.

Soon Harold was driving his car over the boulevards, and together the two chatted of old times. It had been two years since Allan had first touched his feet to Savna soil, and naturally their talk turned to the events that marked his former stay in Magnolia. They spoke of Allan's encounter with Babe Ellis, who, Harold told his friend, had died suddenly. Allan also learned that the brawler whom he had thrown out of the Bishop's house had recovered; learned, too, with sadness that the sheriff's wife had become insane because of the execution of Elsa, whom, as the listener knew, she would have saved if she could.

As they drove slowly along Allan could see no appre-

ciable change since the riot. Some of the houses had
been rebuilt, but in the majority of cases the debris was
still lying untouched on the otherwise vacant lots.

Once Harold spoke of some incident that had
occurred in his invalid days,— an amusing incident
that Allan had forgotten,— which had taken place near
the Bishop's house that still lay there in ashes; whereupon Allan looked at him musingly and asked:

"And you were interested in our affairs even at that
time?"

"Yes," was Harold's eager reply. "I longed for
perfect health that I might have walloped Ellis and his
gang that day; but, of course, I would have cut a sorry
spectacle single-handed during the riot."

While they were thus conversing animatedly they
chanced to meet the Reverend Mr. Stickley and his
daughter, who greeted Harold profusely.

This meeting changed the course of their conversation, and when they started on again Harold happened
to mention his cousin, Donald Bleecker, who lived on
his plantation near the city and who was paying court
to Miss Gertie Stickley.

"And he lives near here?" asked Allan apprehensively.

"Yes; he's a frequent caller at our house."

This information seemed to depress Allan greatly.
Harold noticed the change, though he could not account
for it.

Allan was to remain the guest of the Bleeckers, in
response to Harold's urgent request, during the time
necessary to complete the negotiations that the envoy
of the Decemvirate was pushing with all possible dispatch. It would require at least two weeks to finish
the work.

A week of the time had already passed, yet Allan had seen nothing of Donald Bleecker, though he was quite sure that the former cashier was aware of his presence in Savna.

It was a Saturday morning. Allan had an appointment to keep, after which he and Harold had planned to go fishing together. After finishing his business in the city, he took his way down the shell-road, walking leisurely. Harold, who had started from home with the fishing tackle, caught sight of his black friend approaching slowly in the distance and concealed himself by the roadside in order to surprise Allan.

Taking a book out of his pocket, he sat down in his leafy retreat to await his comrade's coming. He had, however, no soner ensconced himself than he heard someone coming toward him from the opposite direction. Peering out, he saw Gertie Stickley pacing back and forth, apparently waiting for someone. The place was near the secluded spot where Allan had been fired upon,— a depression somewhat resembling an arroya, and screened in by giant trees. Harold wondered if Donald could be coming to join Gertie, wondered, too, why she should wish to meet his cousin so clandestinely.

By this time Allan had reached the crest of the hill and was now slowly descending into the arroya. It was ten o'clock in the morning, and the sun was shining in an unclouded sky. As he came along his way, he noticed the young lady ahead of him. She was in the act of ascending the opposite rise of the little dale, her back being toward him, when a wagon filled with farmers came rapidly in their direction, evidently bound for the city. Without warning, without any apparent cause, Miss Stickly suddenly appeared to be overcome with fright. Putting her hands to her head, she loosened her hair so that it fell about her shoulders and ran screaming toward the advancing team.

"Help! Help!" she cried in terrified accents.

Allan was dumbfounded. He made no effort to either advance or retreat. Then through his senses sounded the words: "I'll git you yet, Mr. Nigger," and he knew that this was the work of Donald Bleecker.

In an instant the men were upon him. They surrounded him; they bound him securely. But no sooner was this accomplished than Harold came upon the scene. He expostulated with the men, told them that he had been a witness of the whole proceeding, and that Allan was innocent of any wrong. He showed them where he had been sitting, explained exactly what had transpired. He talked earnestly with them, pointed out Allan's high standing, vouched for his honor and uprightness, and begged them to release him and not stir up public strife.

Silently the men listened to Harold's fervent plea. At length the silence was broken by one of the men, who said:

"Wall, ef he's innercent, mebbe he kin prove it. But thet's the pastor's dawtah, en' you kin see fer yerself how she wuz actin'."

And after this all Harold's charges of its being a plot and all his pleadings in Allan's behalf were of no avail. They forced their victim to go with them to the city.

Miss Stickley had disappeared as soon as the men had seized Allan, going through the thick woods in the direction of her home.

The news of the alleged assault spread like wildfire. The people began to flock to the city in holiday attire. One would have thought that they were celebrating some festal day. The mayor had ordered the closing of all saloons and had also requested that all places of business suspend operation for that day. In the public square was surging a sea of humanity, brought there in carts, surreys, motorcycles, automobiles, and every other form of conveyance. The lynching had been set for six o'clock, and no reputable citizen of Magnolia would willingly absent himself from the scene.

The Savna *Times* had issued a special edition, bearing a spreadhead on the first page in big, flaming letters, to introduce the thrilling report of the outrage. Jack Carter had " done himself proud " in the accuracy and detail of the description of " the brutal assault." He had flown to dizzy heights in his write-up of his interview with the " poor wounded linnet,"— as he designated the minister's daughter,— as well as in his account of the stolid indifference of her black brute of an assailant.

No excitement marked the temper of the immense throng in the square; nor was there any cursing heard, nor the manifestation of any rowdyism. This was to be a " legal lynching," as one of the denizens of Magnolia was heard to declare. Here and there were boys peddling hokey-pokey ice cream and other confections, while the ladies,— of whom there was an enormous representation,— were munching bon-bons and saying silly nothings to their attendant cavaliers.

Harold had managed to have an interview with Allan, wherein he learned of the radium episode in Cargo City, which had furnished the animus for Donald's betrayal, and he was determined to save his friend's life at all hazards. With this purpose in view, he talked to all the influential men of the city that he could reach, but they all assured him that they were

helpless to interfere. Next he called on the Governor.
This dignitary listened attentively to his story, even did
him the honor of telling him that he believed him, adding:

"But even if I were so disposed, what could I do?
Should I muster an army, my troops would mutiny.
Not a peace officer in all Magnolia would oppose the
will of all the people. You see, my boy, a lady of
Magnolia has been offended,— or at least has com-
plained,— and I fear he could be rescued only by a
miracle."

Even in the face of this discouragement Harold did
not despair. He pressed his mother into service and
requested her to persuade Gertie to withdraw her accu-
sation. Though Mrs. Bleecker did not wish to have
anything to do with the matter, her son's strained features and suppressed emotion made her fear for his
health, so, to please him she sought out Gertie.

The girl admitted that it was a hoax, just as Harold
had said, but added that she was powerless to change
the course of events now. And Mrs. Bleecker elicited
the fact from her that both Donald Bleecker and her
father had told her that it would be out of the question to retract now. Repentant though she was, she
was helpless now that she had been brought to a real-
ization of the tremendous significance of her act.
Nothing could be done.

It was now half-past five in the afternoon, and Allan
had been brought to the public square, where an iron
post had been set up, against which had been heaped
piles of dry wood soaked in tar and kerosene. It was
Allan's funeral pyre, yet he approached it without
flinching.

As they were chaining him to the post a flood of

thoughts swept over him. We have read somewhere
of a Hindu who requested a visitor to place his head in
a tub of water and then withdraw it. On acceding to
the request, the visitor in fancy became a child again,
lived the long intervening years till he had attained
manhood, saw himself married, and watched his children grow to manhood, all within the space of a few
moments. So it was now with Allan. As his bonds
were being made fast, he dwelt on the ancient glory of
his race,— the people of Hamitic type in the land where
history had its bithplace; in memory he traced the con-
quest of those primitive peoples, their national life,
their development, their art, their sculpture, their military achievements, their mighty structures that have
endured the ravages of the ages and which are yet
unequalled by any modern architecture. He thought
of how this glory had departed under the tarnish of
time, and he dwelt, too, on the slough of barbarism
into which his race had sunk because they had failed to
keep pace with civilization.

Again, Allan saw in fancy the inauguration of the
slave trade, the transplanting of his people in a new and
unfriendly land. He thought of their harsh and brutal
masters, of their toil, their privations, their agony, their
patience, their being classed with animals both by law
and custom, the separation of families on the auction
block, and their simple fidelity to their ungrateful
abusers. Then Allan thought of their freedom and the
sanguinary struggle preceding it. He thought that it
was a great step in the progress of civilization to admit,
in theory at least, their rights as men; but a great feeling of resentment arose within his heart when he
remembered their continued oppression. He thought
of the establishment of the Decemvirate, of its steady

growth in money and power, and he uttered a silent prayer for its success. Like all men of great nature, he did not think of himself, except to utter a hope that his martyrdom might help his people to become immune from the torment of this modern barbarism.

And then Allan's thoughts turned to Elsa,— pure, gentle, harmless little Elsa,— Elsa, with her culture, her refinement that showed in every feature, her vivacious yet angelic nature that was always striving to help someone; and all at once a wild, tempestuous rage seized him, and he raised his arms and tore himself loose from his tormentors, throwing a dozen men from their feet. Numerous others rushed upon him and continued the process of binding him. Allan smiled.

Harold, who had just reached the scene after his unsuccessful efforts, mounted the pile of inflammable material and placed himself at Allan's side, from which point he essayed to address the multitude. In an impassioned voice he pleaded that they release Allan, offering to furnish proof of his innocence. Donald Bleecker, who had kept well out of sight, but had mingled freely with the mob, was an interested listener to Harold's remarks. He feared that this earnest champion of his victim might succeed in creating a wave of sentiment in favor of the condemned man, and he hastened toward a small group some distance away that consisted of the Reverend Mr. Stickley, his daughter and Mrs. Bleecker.

Again Harold reiterated his certainty of Allan's innocence and pleaded with the mob to relase him.

" Wall," at length a husky young giant cried, " I tell yuh, boys, we'll bu'n him fust an' investigate this young fellah's tale afterwards."

The District Attorney, who had heard Harold's plea,

now stepped forward. He had been touched by the young man's earnest eloquence.

"Gentlemen," he began, "I think there is something reasonable in what this young man says; and I see no reason why we should not investigate it."

He had gotten this far when Donald Bleecker was seen to whisper to Gertie, his betrothed, and a murmur at once ran through the crowd, which drowned the voice of the District Attorney.

"The lady is coming! The lady is coming!" went the word from mouth to mouth.

Gertie Stickley advanced leaning on Donald Bleecker's arm. As the two reached the base of the funeral pyre, the giant who had recently spoken handed the girl a lighted torch. At the same instant several hands tore Harold Bleecker from the side of Allan Dune. Mrs. Bleecker had fainted.

Allan, standing there bound above her, looked down unemotionally at the young lady, but she dared not meet his gaze. With averted head, she extended her hand, and guided by Donald Bleecker, the torch met a responsive spot in the inflammable pile.

Soon a pyramid of fire was rising — rising heavenward.

On it burned; but not a groan, not a sound, came from the tortured victim; whereat the crowd felt that it had been cheated of half the performance.

Only when the fire was so burnt out that the witnesses could denude the place of every scrap that might serve as a memento,— even to the very ashes,— did the mob slowly disperse.

EPILOGUE

We can only close our narrative with a question: Shall the Decemvirate complete the negotiations inaugurated by Allan Dune and accede to the demands of their insistent contributors, or shall they, because of lack of virility and originality, retrace their steps?

And another: Shall a new civilization spring up over the grave of Elsa Mangus and rise from the ashes of the funeral pyre of Allan Dune?

Patiently we await the answer.

THE END

DATE DUE
